The Teaching Road Map

A Pocket Guide for High School and College Teachers

Nora Haenn and Eric J. Johnson,
with Mary Grace Buckwalter

ROWMAN & LITTLEFIELD EDUCATION
Lanham • New York • Toronto • Plymouth, UK

Published in the United States of America
by Rowman & Littlefield Education
A Division of Rowman & Littlefield Publishers, Inc.
A wholly owned subsidary of The Rowman & Littlefield Publishing Group, Inc.
4501 Forbes Boulevard, Suite 200, Lanham, Maryland 20706
www.rowmaneducation.com

Estover Road
Plymouth PL6 7PY
United Kingdom

British Library Cataloguing in Publication Information Available

Library of Congress Cataloging-in-Publication Data

Haenn, Nora, 1967–
  The teaching road map : a pocket guide for high school and college teachers /
Nora Haenn and Eric Johnson, with Mary Grace Buckwalter.
    p. cm.
  Includes bibliographical references.
  ISBN 978-1-60709-052-6 (cloth : alk. paper) — ISBN 978-1-60709-053-3
(pbk. : alk. paper) — ISBN 978-1-60709-054-0 (electronic)
  1. First year teachers—In-service training. 2. High school teachers—In-service
training. 3. College teachers—In-service training. 4. Teacher orientation.
I. Johnson, Eric, 1974– II. Buckwalter, Mary Grace, 1956– III. Title.
LB2844.1.N4H34 2009
370.71'55—dc22   2009003868

♾ ™ The paper used in this publication meets the minimum requirements of
American National Standard for Information Sciences—Permanence of Paper
for Printed Library Materials, ANSI/NISO Z39.48-1992.
Manufactured in the United States of America.

Contents

Acknowledgments

Nora would like to thank the people who provided great teaching support and advice over the years, including Grace Haenn, Madelaine Adelman, Lisa Cliggett, Peggy Nelson, Ellen Rees, and Kate Spielmann. Also, a number of amazing graduate students at Arizona State University showed a passion for teaching at just the right moment. Their ideas improved the manuscript greatly: Elodie Billionniere, Becki Campanaro, Aimee Ellis, Ann Fletchall, Stacey Flores, Allison Ghan, Jenny Harrison, Catherine MacPherson, Valerye Milleson, Meghna Sabharwal, Tara Schuwerk, Misa Vening, Elle Wolterbeek, Donglin Xia. And, most of all, thanks to Luis Melodelgado who listens to teaching stories at the end of each day.

Eric would like to thank all of his students from Apache Junction High School, the Murphy School District, Mesa Community College, and Arizona State University. Their enthusiasm for learning and openness to new ideas has been very inspirational and motivating. Also, a very special thanks to Bianca Stoll for all of her support and patience over the years.

Introduction

Charting a Course for Successful Teaching

This book was written for those high school and college teachers who arrive on the scene with little practical experience or formal training. New teachers tend to model their classes on their own classroom experiences, a strategy that can turn out to be a bit hit or miss. This book gets new teachers started in establishing their own teaching styles by offering an overview of the most essential points teachers should take into account as they begin their new adventure.

In the spirit of all great road trips, this book looks at a teaching career as a journey. Beginning travelers are likely to be hopeful and excited to see the unknown, anxious to get going, maybe also nervous and concerned about the events for which they may prove unprepared. Anyone who has traveled through a foreign country knows how useful a guide can be in anticipating the unforeseen. Just like that travel book offers tips, maps, dos and don'ts, suggestions, and warnings to help the novice adventurer, our book is designed to be a reliable companion at your side as you embark on your journey as a high school or college instructor. New teachers who have come to the job with little preparation, perhaps a career change brought you to the classroom later in life, will soon learn two keys to teaching success. The first is continued training and the second is tapping into the knowledge of experienced teachers.

This book aims to be a starting point for a more expansive learning. In our writing, we have kept in mind the provisionally trained teacher, including graduate students and PhDs new to the classroom, as well as professionals and others who have recently decided to join the ranks of high school teachers. Even seasoned teaching professionals will find this guide to be a succinct refresher course. We hope that looking at teaching across these settings proves useful for college teachers who want to know something about the environment that shaped their students and for high school teachers who want a better sense of where their students are headed.

As with other travel guidebooks, you can read this one cover to cover or select the chapters of most interest to you. Our brief descriptions allow you to get the most out of each chapter without getting bogged down in details. We also know that some of you might want (or need) more information than we offer here. (Yes, the devil *is* in the details!) This is why we include links to outside resources for further investigation. In keeping with our road map theme, we demonstrate these extras in the form of highly visible road signs. Here's what the road signs look like and what they signify:

Information signs offer avenues for exploring some of the more nuanced topics we discuss. In these signs, we list additional resources such as websites, books, or on-campus locations as starting points for broadening your understanding.

We use caution signs to warn you of possible rough spots along the teaching highway, including common obstacles that you should keep in mind. With foresight, many problems can be easily avoided.

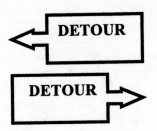

Detour signs appear when we draw on a previously mentioned concept or an idea that is expanded on in later chapters. The detour signs have arrows to indicate whether the information appears in earlier or later chapters.

REST STOP

Rest stops are designed for you to take a few minutes and think about a specific issue. They provide quick strategies for you to apply while you are working. These suggestions include ideas for helping students, organizing your materials, and interacting with your colleagues.

STOP

Stop signs describe suggestions and ideas that we strongly suggest you consider. Most of the situations mentioned here are commonly overlooked but tend to have a strong impact on your teaching.

In addition to the road signs, at the end of each chapter we offer a "to do list" of the most critical steps to take on your journey. These suggestions summarize the chapter's main points. Instead of having to reread each chapter, the "to do lists" can guide you as an overview as you prepare for your classes.

Finally, another tool that we offer is a web-based resource kit. For each chapter, our website has examples, templates, and links to other sources of information. The website also has our contact information in case you need further advice or tips. The site's comment board allows you to post your concerns or success stories for other teachers to see. The website complements the Internet pages we recommend throughout the book. You can find the website at www.theteachingroadmap.com.

As you can see, our approach is based upon getting you the help you need as fast as possible. Whether you teach at a high school, a small liberal arts college, a community college, or a large research university, we offer ideas to fit your situation. We also recognize the differences between secondary and post-secondary settings. Two chapters toward the end of the book address the specifics of high school and college careers. Otherwise, we bridge different kinds of teaching settings by avoiding a one-size-fits-all solution to each context. Instead, we present multiple strategies and techniques from which you can choose.

Our goal is to provide a broad yet substantial framework that will get you through those first years on the job. As you learn the terrain of your new field, your teaching will improve and, likely, demand more specialized teaching guides. We hope that as your learning expands, this book will remain a refreshing reminder of your journey. We just want you to know that—as demanding of a journey as teaching can be—we will be by your side the whole way!

1

Map Your Role in the Classroom

Teaching Philosophies 101

If you're like most new teachers, you might be tempted to skip this first chapter. After all, who needs a teaching philosophy when you're scrambling to pick out books, write a syllabus, and make it through the first day of class? "Hold on a minute," we say. You need a philosophy because your personal approach to the classroom serves as a guide for *why* you choose to structure your class a certain way. Before you type one line of your syllabus, you'll want to ask yourself: "What do I think education is all about? How do I translate my beliefs about education into the students' experience?" Your students may not ever learn the philosophy that led you to create a class as you did; but, with a solid teaching philosophy in hand, you'll approach your students confident that you are contributing to a bigger plan.

BUZZ WORDS IN EDUCATION

If you've already started to work on your teaching philosophy, then you know the field of education has a language all its own. Even the phrase "teaching philosophy" means something specific. It's not a reference to Aristotle, Descartes, or Sartre. Instead, the phrase follows a more colloquial understanding of "philosophy." A teaching philosophy is simply a statement that conveys your basic beliefs about, and attitude toward, teaching. Do a search online for "teaching philosophy," and you'll find essays written by teachers who share their personal vision of what it means to educate and what methods they use to make this vision a reality. These essays make for especially useful models if you need to write a statement of teaching philosophy for a job application. For your own use, your philosophy can be

1

quite simple. One colleague summed up her philosophy in two sentences, "I care. And, I promise not to mess up." Other philosophies we've heard include: "I want to foster learning through hands-on experience." "I want to create thoughtful, inquisitive citizens." "I want to share my passion for the field." "I want my students to have the skills they need to get a job."

In your teaching, you'll encounter more specific models of teaching alongside their complement models of learning. Here, we want to share a few of the more popular approaches. Your own institution or school district may prefer or support certain models of teaching over others. We suggest you check in with your teaching support center or the curriculum and instruction director in your school district to find out which approaches are popular on your campus. (Teaching support centers are great and offer all kinds of help. Don't be shy in asking for their help!) Remember, when it comes to teaching philosophies, the field is wide open. You can mix and match as you like, or develop your own, unique perspective. Your teaching philosophy may change over time. Feel free to throw out a philosophy that isn't working for you and come up with a new one. Let's get started on some of the more popular philosophies with a big-picture question about your teaching.

STUDENT-CENTERED VS. TEACHER-CENTERED INSTRUCTION

If the classroom is a theater, who's on stage? Is the teacher star to an audience of captive students? Or, are the students themselves on stage, and the teacher in the audience? This is the central distinction between teacher-centered and student-centered instruction. You know teacher-centered instruction in its most common form, the lecture. The instructor stands in front of the class dictating information to students (who always sit attentively and take notes, right?). The teacher might throw out an occasional question for discussion only to be met with silence or a response by one of the few students who reliably speak up. In contrast, a visit to a student-centered classroom would reveal an active discussion among the students, either in small or large groups. The instructor walks around guiding conversations by prompting questions and offering other points of view. Is one of these approaches better than the other? Why or why not? For the moment, our interest is in student-centered versus teacher-centered instruction as *teaching philosophies*. So, we'll set aside for now the practical implications of the two approaches.

You might argue that the teacher-centered classroom is a better approach because students learn best from an expert in the field who acts as a guide to the subject matter. Perhaps your teaching philosophy emphasizes your role in sharing field-specific knowledge that students could not otherwise access on their own. Maybe the subject area you teach is ethically fraught and you want to be able to delineate the field carefully so student encounters with the material are more sophisticated.

A teacher-centered approach can make especially good sense when an instructor's knowledge is somehow unmatched. There really are "star" teachers out there; people whose innovations changed their field, inspired their colleagues, and won them acclaim. Students will flock to these educators in order to learn at the feet of a master. Unfortunately, your authors are not (yet!) these kinds of instructors. And, our own teaching philosophies tend to favor student-centered over teacher-centered classes. Still, we see a place for teacher-centered classrooms when they fit an educator's larger goals and personal style. Many classrooms are a mix of the two styles for the benefit of diverse student learning styles. In later chapters, we offer tips to improve student experiences in teacher-centered classrooms.

Student-centered philosophies build on the idea that people learn best by doing something for themselves. A brief example will show you what we mean. As a small child, you might have hovered around the kitchen stove while someone was cooking. "Don't touch that pot. It's hot," said the responsible grown-up. But, you touched it anyway. Which do you remember better, being told the pot was hot, or feeling the burning sensation? We don't suggest your students should suffer in their learning, but you see what we mean.

Sometimes there's just no substitute for personal experience. We know this from another adage: We remember 20 percent of what we hear, 50 percent of what we see, but 80 percent of what we do. A class that builds on student-centered teaching philosophies will seek ways to include experience in students' education through hands-on activities, a field trip, or laboratory work. The idea here is that even with access to all the knowledge and skills of the world's top experts, many students will still learn more about your field of study through direct observation and participation.

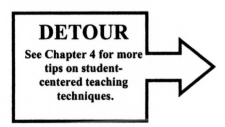

DETOUR
See Chapter 4 for more tips on student-centered teaching techniques.

The debate over student-centered and teacher-centered instruction has a long history in the field of education. Many college professors, having spent their own careers in a lecture hall, start out teacher-centered and find themselves to be more student-centered as time goes by. In a university context, instructors assigned large classes of hundreds of students may have little choice but to deliver a traditional lecture. In any case, deciding whether your classes will be teacher-centered, student-centered, or some combination of the two is just a beginning. The choice conveys the overall shape of your course. The following theories of *learning* provide direction for the course's content. Again, the idea here is that your beliefs about teaching, that is, your teaching philosophy, may arise out of your understanding of how learning takes place.

CONSTRUCTIVISM AND ZONE OF PROXIMAL DEVELOPMENT (ZPD)

Don't be put off by the jargon. These two approaches actually have an intuitive feel about them. Both approaches espouse the idea that people use previously acquired knowledge and experience to make sense of new concepts. That is, people learn by building on what they already know. Constructivism views this existing knowledge as located in the student's head. ZPD views this existing knowledge as located within the student's social world.

Constructivism lies behind teaching tactics that start out with students' own experiences and then move on to more abstract and unfamiliar ground. The idea here is that by drawing on students' common knowledge base when introducing new ideas you allow them both to absorb the information and understand it more effectively. Because of this, a constructivist approach to teaching views the teacher's job as one of unearthing existing knowledge and predispositions in order to locate the student's path to more sophisticated understandings.

Here's a brief example of a constructivist approach to teaching. Say you want to teach students a concept like democracy. A constructivist teacher would first ask students to define democracy for themselves, informally, using whatever notions that pop into their minds. Students might say things like "voting in an election," "a system of government used in the United States," and so on. Your notion of democracy might be more formal than this, but you can build on what students have to offer. Yes, democracy entails voting in elections. At the same time, some theories of democracy expand citizens' roles to include participation in public debate. Yes, the United States government operates on democratic principles, as do the governments of countries that, in practice, look very different from the United States, such as parliamentary democracies. From this discussion, the constructivist teacher can go on to more abstract discussions, always building upon prior knowledge. What would the political theorist John Dewey say about voting as a form of public deliberation? What does Habermas' theory of the public sphere say about voting? In making these jumps, the constructivist teacher is careful to bring students along and to demonstrate how one piece of information builds on another.

INFO

Interested in learning more about constructivism? Head over to:

http://carbon.cudenver.edu/~mryder/itc_data/constructivism.html

---

ZPD is constructivism in its social form. ZPD argues that people learn best in social settings where they build on other people's experiences in undertaking the same task. ZPD has its roots in the work of Russian psychologist Lev Vygotsky. Vygotsky noticed that children often observe adults doing different tasks and gradually develop the ability to do the same tasks without assistance. The base of learning that children build on exists in the social world that surrounds them. Vygotsky termed the difference between what a child can do with assistance and what a child can do without guidance as the "zone of proximal development" or the ZPD.

INFO

For more background on Vygotsky, visit:

http://starfsfolk.khi.is/solrunb/vygotsky.htm

A teaching philosophy based on Vygotsky's ZPD might result in a class where students are grouped together according to varied levels of ability. For example, a teacher might form small groups in which students with stronger capabilities work with students whose skills need improvement. According to ideas of ZPD, small group discussion would then create a "scaffold of information," as students themselves elaborate a concept or task from its simplest form to more complex levels. Skilled students benefit from the arrangement by teaching to unskilled students—connecting to the idea that teaching can be the best form of learning. Unskilled students benefit from the model offered by their more advanced peers.

```
┌─────────────────────────────────────────────┐
│                    INFO                       │
│                                               │
│    Check out how some schools link multiple   │
│    courses to foster constructivist learning: │
│                                               │
│  http://wac.colostate.edu/aw/articles/luebke_2002.htm │
└─────────────────────────────────────────────┘
```

ZPD approaches to teaching are often used in foreign language classrooms, where students have different language abilities. Seminar discussions, where students apply diverse theories to a single phenomenon, are
also good sites to employ ZPD. As with constructivism, the teacher working
in a ZPD style wants to make sure the learning path is clear. In this case,
the teacher focuses attention on how members of a student group model
learn for one another.

STEPS IN LEARNING

Over the years, education theorists have gone beyond the constructivist and
ZPD approaches to describe learning as something that takes place within
a series of hierarchical steps. We want to mention here that you shouldn't
think of the following lists as rigid steps, nor are we implying that students
at lower levels are intellectually deficient. Instead, it is important to realize
that students pass through these levels at different paces. Some students
skip steps or jump around on the scale. Other students may excel at lower
levels (such as memorization) in ways that obscure their difficulties at
higher levels. For the purpose of developing your teaching philosophy, being familiar with these steps in learning provides a good guide for thinking
about your goals in the classroom.

In his description of an educational setting, Benjamin Bloom categorized
different types of problem-solving skills into a taxonomy that moves toward
increasing levels of abstraction. Bloom's Taxonomy has proven very popular over the years and it's probably the hierarchy teachers most commonly
cite. Six of the basic learning steps described by the taxonomy include:

1. Knowledge: observation and recall of information
2. Comprehension: understanding information
3. Application: using information
4. Analysis: seeing patterns
5. Synthesis: using old ideas to create new ones
6. Evaluation: comparing and discriminating between ideas

> ## INFO
> **For an expanded description of Bloom's Taxonomy, check out:**
> www.coun.uvic.ca/learn/program/hndouts/bloom.html

Understanding how to apply Bloom's approach in your own classroom can serve as a basis for your teaching philosophy. Your philosophy might say: "I want to facilitate student learning at higher levels of abstraction." For example, a teacher employing Bloom's Taxonomy could structure tasks that, first, demonstrate comprehension, then application, then analysis, and so on. This approach could require students revisit the same body of information—an article, a book, a dataset—with different intentions. An even broader application might include structuring different courses around different skill levels. In your introductory classes, you might want to emphasize assignments around the knowledge, comprehension, and application levels. For an upper-division course, you can strive toward analysis, synthesis, and evaluation.

Another influential theory that complements Bloom's Taxonomy is Howard Gardner's idea of multiple intelligences. According to Gardner, most people can be categorized as having one (or more) of the following types of intelligences:

1. Linguistic (good with words)
2. Logical-Mathematical (good with numbers and reasoning)
3. Spatial (good with pictures and designs)
4. Bodily-Kinesthetic (good with body movements)
5. Musical (musically inclined)
6. Interpersonal (good with people and relationships)
7. Intrapersonal (good relating with oneself)
8. Naturalist (appreciates and knows nature)

For the educator working from Gardner's philosophy, the trick is to structure activities that tap into a variety of learning styles. Very likely, you'll hear about this listing from your own students, when they say, "I'm a visual learner." In today's media-saturated world, many students assume they are visual learners. In actuality, you will have students from most of these categories and, while most people stand out in one of the categories, very few are limited to a single type of intelligence.

How do you create a class that taps into your students' multiple intelligences? Some teachers advocate setting out clay for students to toy with

while class is underway. These same teachers are interested in students'
bodily-kinesthetic intelligence. Even if students are confined to a desk, the
teacher might want to allow students a physical outlet, say in doodling or
fidgeting. Students who are good interpersonal learners may not be able
to resist the urge to talk to the person next to them. Teachers espousing a
multiple-intelligence philosophy recognize that often students are talking
about the material at hand and aren't too bothered by brief student asides.
And what about that beautiful spring day that has everyone longing to be
outdoors? While the occasional outdoor classroom is good for cabin fever,
it might also help the naturalist in your class.

> ## INFO
>
> **If you'd like to see a little more on
> Gardner's theory, hit up:**
>
> http://www.infed.org/thinkers/gardner.htm

One of our favorite multiple-intelligence activities is to have students
report on a topic using their strongest skill. The student chooses the skill.
We got the idea from someone who recalled the same assignment in a class
on Shakespeare. He was an art student who didn't even want to be in the
class. The assignment motivated him, and he responded by turning Hamlet
into a comic book. It was a class he remembered thirty years after the fact.
Typically, teachers reach out to one or two learning styles, usually linguistic
and/or logical-mathematical. But, you can present your material so that
everyone gets a chance to experience it in his or her own way. The teaching
philosophy known as "universal design" takes this idea a step further by
taking into account physical and learning disabilities.

Universal design operates on the idea that instructors will guarantee all
students access to course material, period. Students with hearing difficulties
need not worry about listening to a lecture, as written notes will be available. Students with limited mobility need not worry about a class field trip,
as the instructor will make sure the transportation and field site accommodate wheel chairs or students on crutches. Universal design often requires
you to duplicate your material across a variety of media—print, voice,
physical activity, and so on. While originally developed to smooth the way
for students with disabilities, universal design can significantly deepen all
of your students' understanding, while simultaneously cultivating their
other (maybe latent) types of intelligences. Duplication of materials gives
students with different types of intelligences the chance to shine in the
classroom because each has had a fair starting point.

Teachers adopting a multiple-intelligence or universal-design perspective often build into their philosophy the goal of having students appreciate physical, cultural, and social differences. The idea here is to use students' differences to enhance their learning while simultaneously educating students about those same differences. The hope is that, in doing so, students will do more than accept each other's abilities and contributions; they will celebrate human diversity.

INFO

Interested in more on Universal Design? Swing by:
www.udeducation.org/

Whichever teaching philosophy you choose, you can add to it the notion of making the learning path transparent to students. Regardless of the subject matter, you might want to explain to students how specific assignments operate at a certain level of knowledge, which levels come next, and even which levels might not be addressed in your class. For example, high school students receive strong training in knowledge and comprehension, allowing you to use Bloom's Taxonomy to shape a syllabus that emphasizes knowledge application. The transparent part comes in when you say to students, "I know you are all trained in memorization. This class takes you to the next level as we put memorized ideas into action." With multiple intelligences and universal design, you can encourage students to explore different ways of learning and allow them to reflect upon what the different approaches have to offer them.

By carefully situating your teaching within a particular path and by illuminating that path to your students, you facilitate the development of the ideal student: the independent, self-directed learner who identifies her or his shortcomings and works to overcome them. While Bloom's Taxonomy, multiple intelligences, and universal design all offer a path to learning around which you can build a teaching philosophy, you might consider deepening these approaches further so that they fit your own personal goals and views on education.

WHAT LEVEL OF LEARNING CAN STUDENTS REASONABLY ACHIEVE?

While the learning theories apply to any person of any age, they tend to have a stronger presence in high schools, raising the question: Can we adapt these to college settings and high school students working at advanced levels? The answer, as always, depends upon the student. Nonetheless, a number of highly skilled teachers are beginning to combine the various approaches we've reviewed thus far to come up with a more general way of thinking about learning. Here's our rough guide to this comprehensive approach. Given its newness, this approach has yet to be boiled down into a few simple steps (although we try below) nor does it have a catchy title. Still, we like this plan because it retains a feel for teaching that is closer to how things seem to work in practice.

This view of learning begins with those students who just want to be told the right answer to a question. We're not talking about the "just-tell-me-what-I-need-to-know-for-the-exam" kind of student, the ones motivated by their grades. We're talking here about students who honestly think that every question has one correct answer. These students have only learned to memorize simple facts. When you present them with other forms of learning and other kinds of knowledge, they stumble. These students may be incoming freshman or they may be students majoring in other fields who are unfamiliar with how your discipline handles contradiction and controversy. According to this new theory of education, the first step in student learning rests on getting beyond the simplistic notion that all questions have just one answer.

How do students get out of this rut? By acknowledging there is no single, correct answer, by working with *uncertainty* in knowledge. A classic way undergraduates go about this is by taking courses that emphasize how a topic or theory appears different depending upon the perspective of the observer. Introduction to sociology classes excel in this approach. But, getting students to recognize a diversity of perspectives is not always an easy task. Students working with uncertainty, but not yet capable of incorporating diverse perspectives into their thinking, may argue based on opinion, use evidence selectively, and jump to conclusions. They may acknowledge other perspectives, only to refute them.

Notice, this philosophy includes some less than intellectually satisfying steps on the path to higher learning. Each step forward carries with it an associated obstacle (see chart below). By acknowledging these obstacles as necessary and transitional—although you may not want to reward them—you will ease your level of stress and frustration. With solid faculty guidance, better things await the student!

REST STOP

Don't be frustrated by student setbacks. Remember, some kinds of stumbling are a natural part of the learning process.

In this case, teachers work with students to accept the inherent uncertainty in knowledge, so students cope with and recognize multiple perspectives on a topic. As time goes by, students may come to view this multiplicity as key to their own understanding. They will be unsatisfied with single answers to a question, and they will seek out complexity. The messiness associated with this stage comes about as students struggle with bias, both their own and that of the authors they read. Their investigations end with, "It all depends. . . ." Robert Rotenberg, an advocate of the new college learning, describes what happens once students begin to explore diverse viewpoints. "Students are often blocked . . . [by] the increased weight of evidence they must sift through . . . Unable to formulate a coherent conclusion[,] their papers are long and tend to ramble. These students do not want to stop analyzing" (20–21). The solution to this obstacle lies in the next stage, prioritizing information.

Prioritizing information is the kind of learning typical of independent research, a senior thesis, or capstone course in a student's major. Prioritizing tends to take place as a natural result of a heavy workload. Teachers send students off to examine an unwieldy amount of information and require they return with some summary of what they find. This task forces students to prioritize because they cannot accomplish the goal without cutting corners. As they prioritize, students often seek out strategic collaborations to winnow out inappropriate material. They might find a new appreciation for librarians or, in schools with graduate programs, seek the advice of graduate students. All in all, they begin to make judgments about the quality of information, so they can ignore less helpful sources.

While certainly a more advanced stage in learning, prioritizing information is not without its own messiness. Teachers who emphasize too much a final product—a paper or a presentation—might miss rewarding the process of complex investigation. In order to assess whether and how well a student is prioritizing, faculty must ask: "How did the student sift through information to establish a thesis and defend that thesis with appropriate evidence?"

The creation of a thesis with appropriate evidence—the outcome of accepting uncertainty, acknowledging multiple perspectives, controlling for bias, and prioritizing information—is about as far as most college students get in their learning, although there are two more steps to go in the schema. These latter steps are typical of graduate students and grad school–bound undergraduates. They include immersion into a particular area of study, and the transformation of a student into what we call a self-starter, someone who is self-motivated, who continues to learn on their own without much prompting.

Here's a recap of the stages of learning as outlined by this new approach to education, alongside their messy, transitional phases. Remember, each

Table 1.1.   Phases of Student Inquiry

Phase	*Transition*
Searches for a single, correct answer	Is demotivated by not knowing the right answer
Accepts uncertainty by acknowledging multiple perspectives	Can't stop analyzing the different perspectives; gets trapped in "It depends . . . "
Prioritizes information	As with the above, may happen in slow, incomplete steps
Creates thesis (out of multiple perspectives) with appropriate evidence	
Immersion in a knowledge base	Immensity of material raises anew problems in handling multiple perspectives and prioritizing
Seeks continuous self-improvement in knowledge without prompting	

transition may be a necessary or typical path toward the next, higher-level phase.

As a teaching philosophy, this approach imagines a classroom that employs something like the Socratic method, where educators pose complex problems that can only be resolved by exploring a variety of angles. Laboratory settings that require a series of experiments to address the same topic are great ways to have students explore how contradictory steps can contribute to problem solving. Interestingly, this approach argues for purposefully assigning advanced students more material than they can handle as long as the assignments require prioritizing (outlining your goal here will forestall any pushback from students).

As with Bloom's Taxonomy, this approach to education emphasizes intellectual development. So maybe you're wondering, "Are people all head and no heart?" Is there more to learning than what takes place in the student's mind? As we saw, ideas of multiple intelligences and universal design make steps toward a teaching philosophy that is more than brain focused. Paradoxically, the theory that takes the most steps in this regard is known as "brain-based learning."

BRAIN-BASED LEARNING

Despite its name, "brain-based learning" works to take into account the emotional aspect of student progress. In this way, the concept is similar to experiential education. Both philosophies approach learning as part of a broader setting. In the case of brain-based learning, teachers work with the emotional tone of the classroom to facilitate learning. Many of the teaching tips in later chapters—especially classroom management—aim to put brain-based learning into action. Optimally, instructors working in a brain-based tradition will design lessons around three basic premises:

Table 1.2. Premise of Brain-Based Learning

1. Orchestrated immersion	Educators create a classroom that includes lots of hands-on activities and visual stimuli;
2. Relaxed alertness	Instructors establish an environment of reduced anxiety and heightened excitement toward participation;
3. Active processing	Teachers give students the opportunity to use or demonstrate what they have learned.

Brain-based learning may seem obvious to you. Clearly, teachers should create a classroom in which students are safe to voice their thoughts and make intellectual explorations. As instructors, we shouldn't be condescending, cold, or judgmental. A closer look shows that brain-based learning takes the idea of a safe classroom to a higher level by suggesting that teachers put that safety to use in student learning. A teaching philosophy based on a brain-based perspective would spend considerable classroom time building community both among students and between students and teacher. The teacher would then work with this foundation to convey subject matter and make it more comfortable for students to stretch themselves in the field. The goal here simply is one of mutual respect in an alert, yet relaxed, hands-on environment.

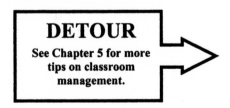

DETOUR
See Chapter 5 for more tips on classroom management.

SO, WHAT'S YOUR TEACHING PHILOSOPHY?

In the end, the most important determiner of your teaching philosophy is your own experience. Identifying and exploiting your personal style is the most important task you face as a new teacher. What motivates you to teach? Beyond conveying your subject matter, what's your overall goal for your teaching? What count as best teaching practices for you? Do you think students learn best when grouped with people of different abilities, the ZPD approach? Or, do students learn best when you tap into their different forms of intelligence, the universal design- or multiple-intelligences approaches? Will students be listening to your lectures, or will they be exploring case studies and independent learning exercises? Have you already taught and, perhaps, learned you're a fantastic lecturer, even though your personal inclination is toward experiential learning?

INFO

Check out these sites for some ideas on classroom icebreakers and community building:

www.education-world.com/a_lesson/lesson/lesson131.shtml
www.eslflow.com/ICEBREAKERSreal.html

Some educators become passionate about a particular teaching philosophy. You'll find some philosophies work better in some institutions than in others. Some classes and material lend themselves to certain philosophies (think of the case study methods used in medicine), while others are quite flexible. As a beginning teacher, you might find much here that excites you, but don't feel like you have to be all things to all people. In crafting your own teaching philosophy, draw on your existing strengths. Work to reach the greatest number of students, but know that it's okay to draw some lines. If you're allergic to sports and never happier than on your couch engrossed in a novel, then don't feel the need to structure a kinesthetic classroom. That's just not what you're about. As you explore new approaches in small doses, your students will see that you care about your teaching style and their learning. Which, after all, isn't a bad teaching philosophy.

TO DO LIST

1. Identify what motivates you to teach.
2. Identify your strengths & weaknesses as a teacher.
3. Combine your motivations & best teaching practices to come up with a teaching philosophy that reflects your personal style.
4. Sketch out your ideas on paper in preparation for writing a more formal statement of your teaching philosophy.

2

Choose Your Materials

Readings, Activities, and Movies 101

Selecting effective materials for your course is the most important step to ensure an effective and well-organized class. We know, you're probably asking yourself: "What about the syllabus?" But you need to keep in mind that all assignments, tests, and activities should reflect the materials that you choose for your students. The flow of classroom instruction and your students' interest level depend upon how you present ideas to them through the activities you structure. There's nothing worse than having to use materials that you know will bore your students to death (except maybe using something that bores you to death!).

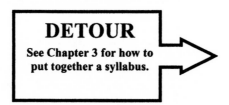

DETOUR
See Chapter 3 for how to put together a syllabus.

Even though high school teachers are usually given a predetermined textbook and ancillary materials (e.g., worksheets and tests), rarely do these cover everything you want to discuss in class. Most high school teachers have the option to choose materials that will enrich or supplement their curriculum. College professors usually have the freedom to select meaningful materials for both you and your students—but, in choosing your own materials, you can't blame anyone else if your materials don't adequately engage your students. In this section, we will touch on some basic strategies for selecting readings, movies, activities, and other instructional materials.

SELECTING YOUR MATERIALS

First, let's go over some general tips. Getting your hands on the readings and previewing them is always best. Depending upon your time frame, this might not be possible (don't worry, we'll cover that scenario, too). But, by previewing, you avoid shocking surprises. One of us served as a teaching assistant for an introductory class in cultural anthropology whose first day proved a bit distracting by a movie exuberantly describing the joy of new life, complete with a close-up of a human birth! It was a first impression of a teacher and a class that could have been avoided with a preview. A rule of thumb is to have no more than 25 percent of your assignments include material you haven't had time to preview. At the high school level, even this amount might be too much as teachers will ultimately be answerable to a school board should the materials present a problem.

REST STOP

Make your previewing a little easier and more enjoyable. Pull together a peer group that can work together on this and other teaching duties.

As you introduce this new material, teach your class to examine the assignment critically. If the material wins over the students then you know it's a keeper! If not, you can praise the class for their critical eye.

Advance copies of books, movies, and other course materials are available from the publishing companies—just make sure to order them at least two or three months before you actually need them. In the case of movies, some companies will let you rent before buying. To find the most current films in distribution, you should try sources like publishers' distribution lists, *Amazon*.com, or the local libraries. High school teachers will have access to a state regional education service that can also act as a resource for you. As for selecting your materials, here are some other helpful ways to start the previewing process.

A great place to peruse the latest offerings in your field is professional conferences. The book exhibits don't include just books. You'll find movies, website advertisings, and book company representatives who can show you the latest supporting materials they already offer for their texts. Professional meetings often dedicate special sessions to the newest films in your area. These are movies that may not be in distribution but touch on the most up-to-date topics in your field. At conferences, you can try out ideas on your colleagues, quiz them about materials they've used, and get a better sense of how particular selections work in practice. High school teachers might pledge to attend at least two workshops or conferences a year outside your school district in order to pick up ideas overlooked in your immediate circle of colleagues.

The Internet may be the first place you turn for help finding materials, but remember all those materials online will be better at telling you what's supposed to happen, not how it actually happens in practice. Use the Web for overall information—textbooks, bibliographies, course outlines, lesson plans, lab manuals, movie ideas, and so on—but don't rely on the Web to preview materials. You still need to personally make sure they are engaging and appropriate for what you have in mind.

If the clock is ticking and you don't have a lot of time before classes begin, don't panic, there are still a few options left. First, ask around your department and see if your colleagues can lend you a copy of books with which they have had success. If there is a particularly interesting book that you want to review, check area libraries. If you don't have time to review complete texts, you can always use selected journal articles and book chapters for your class. We cover how to select and organize these types of readings below. In case of a time-crunch emergency (we stress *emergency*), you can always pick short readings as you go along, according to the topics being covered in class. Be forewarned, this tactic can be very stressful for both you and your students. Not knowing what you are going to teach each week usually ends up in a lot of last-minute preparation for you, and a lot of complaints from the students.

High school teachers often have the liberty to order supplementary materials for class (e.g., movies, novels, magazines). Before you do this, you need to discuss your ideas with your department chairperson. If she or he likes your proposal, you will need to place a purchase order through that chairperson or an administrator (usually an assistant principal). Be forewarned, these orders may be made as long as two years in advance of a course offering, but discretionary funds may only be available for a more immediate purchase. In some cases, you might need to write up an official proposal of why you want to include your preferred book or movie in your class. You might even have to present your idea to the school board. Regardless of the bureaucracy involved, don't be intimidated by the chain of command. If a particular book motivates you, go through the official steps to get it in your students' hands!

Once you have rounded up all your course materials, there are some final details that you need to consider. First, is it plausible to cover all of the material you're considering in one semester, quarter, or school year? Ask around your department and see how much reading other teachers usually assign (as well as how much they think their students should be able to handle; often the amounts are very different). Second, exactly, how many hours of homework do other teachers in your school expect? Is there a policy regarding homework? Schools where most of the students can dedicate their full time to studying can ask a bit more of their students. If most of your students are working, taking a limited load, or have weaker studying skills, you might need to ease up a little.

Closely related to this question of time is whether the amount of reading, writing, and other exercises you're considering is appropriate for your course level and the number of credits being offered. In post-secondary schools, professors tend to expect more of their upper-division students—usually their majors—but other than this rough guideline, much is left to the educator's discretion. In high schools, homework may also be dependent upon the course level; advanced placement (AP) students will be doing more homework than basic-level students. Figure out the range of workloads assigned to introductory, mid-range, and advanced students at your school and adjust your expectations accordingly. If your colleagues don't have a rule of thumb for this, you'll find the information you need embedded in the syllabi they use.

CAUTION

Assigning material that is too
advanced will likely result in
student frustration and,
ultimately, their disinterest.

In addition to the amount of material you assign, you need to consider the difficulty of what you're asking of your students. The learning theories outlined in chapter 1 will help you in this regard. As time goes by, you'll be able to figure out, generally, where your students are on the high school or college learning curve and monitor or adjust your material to the appropriate level. In the meantime, there may be a few shortcuts that, in the least, let you know you're not assigning graduate-level work to undergraduates, or AP-level assignments to basic-level sophomores (typical miscalculations for new teachers).

If you aren't sure about the reading level required for a particular text, some websites can calculate the approximate grade level of a book by simply analyzing a paragraph or two. Otherwise you have a few options. You might ask veteran teachers to show you the syllabi they've used over the course of their careers. Ask to see a few examples of their most effective syllabi, as well as one that didn't work out so well. The Internet can also be a source for course curricula similar to your own. Many school districts, teachers, universities, and professors now post these online.

> ## INFO
> **The *SMOG Reading Level Calculator* is just a click away:**
> **www.harrymclaughlin.com/SMOG.htm**

For college instructors, a comparison with other syllabi proves more important. Nationally, college instructors have reached an informal consensus regarding what material belongs where in the curriculum. A review of syllabi from institutions similar to your own will give you the confidence that you're asking neither too little nor too much. Here, you'll want to be careful the syllabi reflect your own school (community college, liberal arts, or other) and time constraints (semester, quarter system, or intersession class).

DETOUR
See Chapter 3 for more info on developing course objectives.

Once you have figured out a rough picture of what you want to assign, and you have a sense that the amount of the material and the content is appropriate for your class setting, take a step back and examine how well the materials you've chosen flow together. Are the materials supportive of one another topically? Methodologically? Are you asking the students to make big leaps in topic and method? Or, do you foresee smooth transitions? Some educators argue that, regardless of the subject matter, students can usually master two, maybe three, new skills in the course of a term. Prioritize those skills and knowledge you want your students to learn and avoid material that distracts from—rather than adds to or deepens—your main points. As the teaching philosophies showed, by revisiting material with different intentions, students can deepen their learning.

CAUTION

If you need to reserve any library materials or media equipment, like movies or a projector, request them well in advance.

Finally, if your students will be buying materials, think about the cost of what you assign. Cash-strapped students will avoid buying expensive books they suspect are a waste of money, ultimately missing out on what you are trying to teach. Set a reasonable budget for your class and stick to it. Sometimes, we list book prices on our syllabi. We note the list price and the used book prices, so students can see we care about their finances. Lower-income students can benefit from texts and other materials placed on reserve in the school library. If you use the library, make sure students can use the text for a limited but reasonable amount of time, so it remains available to everyone.

ORDERING YOUR MATERIALS

Okay, now it is time to order your materials. Usually, ordering takes place through an administrative assistant in the head office of your department or directly through a campus bookstore. We also know college instructors who support independent and specialty bookstores by placing their orders off campus. In either case, be aware of book order deadlines. If you are late getting the order in, you might not have your books on time. Nothing rattles your preparation like knowing that your students won't have access to the texts until "sometime" in the next weeks. At the high school level, books are usually ordered in the summer—though, be aware that your materials might not make it to you until the winter. Ask about and get to know your district and bookstore protocols.

STOP

College teachers: Always check your book orders at the campus book store a day or two before class starts. Ordering mistakes happen.

College students are increasingly ordering books on their own through the Web. The online prices tend to be best, but we suggest you don't rely on web purchases. The timing can be sketchy, and, as the teacher, it's your responsibility to provide reliable access to the materials you require.

What if all the ordering deadlines have passed and school is just about to start? As a last resort, talk with the bookstore or department staff in charge of ordering. Give them a few book options and ask which can arrive in the shortest time. Place your order then revisit your syllabus and create writing or hands-on assignments to carry the class until the materials arrive. These should be pedagogically useful exercises with close connections to your topic. Think carefully about how you will integrate the exercises with the course materials when they do arrive. Finally, just to protect yourself, expect the materials to take longer to arrive than planned. Plot an extra week without your materials just to be on the safe side.

TEXTBOOKS

One reason there are so many textbooks on the market is that rarely will you find a teacher who loves everything about a particular text (excluding the authors, of course). Instructors often complain about the organization of the material, its lack of relevancy to students' lives, confusing or dry language, and the need for more depth in specific areas. Even though these criticisms might be true, textbooks are a nice guide, even a safety blanket for students, and they can be a good tool for beginning educators. Until you gain experience and know exactly what you want to teach, textbooks offer an array of helpful material.

INFO

Need some help evaluating a textbook? Visit:

www.kutztown.edu/library/materials/textbookevaluation.pdf

While some departments may require you use a certain textbook (covered below), many give you the liberty to find your own. When looking for an appropriate textbook, ask yourself a few simple questions. To begin with, is it well written and easy to read? Run a paragraph or two through an online reading-level calculator tool like the one we mention above. Your students will lose interest quickly if they can't stay awake while reading it, but some boredom can be avoided through well-written texts that offer colorful graphics. If you can, ask some students to read the text and tell you what they thought of it.

REST STOP

Teach your students how to stay awake while reading:

- change reading positions
- walk around every ~15 minutes
- read with a friend and talk about the passage
- read with a pen or pencil, underline, take notes

Next, consider a few key questions. How much of the text will you actually use? If you assign just one-third or one-half of the text, students will wonder if they got their money's worth. How well does the text cover your areas of expertise? While you may not be intimately familiar with all of the topics covered in the book, if you're unhappy with how it treats your field then you might not want to use it. Students question instructors who teach against a text, so make sure, overall, you don't feel the need to contradict the books you assign. Does the text provide supplemental information and activities (e.g., anecdotes, definitions, links to the Internet, CD-ROM activities, study guides, or test banks)? These types of materials can significantly increase the students' understanding of the material and offer opportunities for in-class activities. If the book doesn't include these kinds of options, it should at least offer a handful of starting points for group discussions (e.g., questions at the back of the chapter and thought-provoking statements).

If you are stuck with a book that you come to dislike (either an accidental selection or a book you were directed to use by your department), there are ways to work around this problem.

- First, ask other instructors who have used the book about strategies that have worked for them and their classes. This is especially important if the text is a departmental assignment. Your fellow faculty may have already worked through the problems you're encountering.
- Second, choose the book's sections you think work best and supplement these with outside readings.
- Third, if the authors make statements with which you don't agree, highlight these as examples of different perspectives within your discipline. Create a series of class debates that ask students to weigh the evidence for and against particular viewpoints.
- Fourth, if the book is hard for students to understand and requires a lot of background reading, divide your class into groups and have individual teams prepare background presentations or papers that are available to everyone.

In general, you can work with a flawed textbook by turning the text into an object for student analysis. Have the students summarize, critique, and offer opinions about the text's contents. In large classes, have the students undertake this work in group activities to provide in-depth discussion, peer learning, and ease of assessment. You may find the text's flaws have a hidden benefit in developing students' learning skills.

STOP

Try writing down comments in the margins and mark pages with *Post-It* notes, so you can quickly come up with examples if anyone asks you why you don't like the book.

TOPIC-SPECIFIC BOOKS

As you gain more experience, you might not want to use a textbook. If you are teaching an upper-level or content-specific course, a textbook for your topic may not even exist. More than likely, in these situations, you'll want to include a series of articles or topic-specific books that include primary materials and scholarly productions. Since deciding on your course material can be a lengthy process, you should always start out by asking yourself: "Why am I picking this?" Usually, teachers choose material based on prize-winning research, the author's reputation, or the material's current popularity among other instructors. New instructors often assign the books and materials that most excited them to study their topic. Relying on the prominent material in your area—again, if it offers an appropriate level for your classes—is always a safe strategy.

Topic-oriented edited volumes provide a good variety of readings for your students as well as material for extended research projects that you might want to assign. As with textbooks, make sure that if you require an edited volume you utilize as many of the readings as possible. If you think only one or two of the readings really apply to your course, consider using a class reading packet (see below).

JOURNAL ARTICLES

While some instructors like to supplement their readings with journal articles, others base their entire course around them. If you are planning on assigning journal articles, you need to be aware of copyright infringement laws. Whether or not your use infringes someone else's copyright depends on a number of factors, including how much of the original material you use, why you use it, and what effect your usage has on the ability of the copyright owners to market their publication. The law is not cut-and-dried, so look online for a copyright questionnaire that helps you assess whether your use violates the law.

Once you have cleared up any copyright concerns and organized your reading assignments, contact the school's bookstore or local copy shop. Many will produce a bound packet for the students after having first confirmed you are within the copyright laws. Copiers also will include the extra costs associated with copyright credit in the price of the packet, which can make for an expensive course reader. Be sure the finances are worth it before committing to specific materials for your class.

Additional ways of offering students articles involve online editions of journals (students aren't charged for access!), electronic texts, and journal databases. School libraries all subscribe to certain databases and electronic materials, and some libraries will allow an instructor to bring a class in to

INFO

For more background on copyright infringement laws, here's a good spot to explore:
www.utsystem.edu/OGC/intellectualProperty/copypol2.htm

Here's a copyright wizard will walk you through your situation step by step:
www.benedict.com/Info/FairUse/FairUseWizard.aspx

preview materials. (The size of your class will matter here.) You can also create your own, mini-library either in an online format (like Blackboard) or in your department. Some departments include a place where students can check out class articles. This tactic frees you from having to make photocopies for everyone in the class by giving students the responsibility for making their own personal copies (for large classes, you should provide multiple master copies). Be aware, though, the mini-library can be a hassle for the students. They tend to want access to the articles at the same time. Inevitably, a few students arrive to class unprepared because they couldn't get a hold of the readings. Regardless of how you make them available, journal articles and selected readings are an excellent means of expanding on important ideas.

FILMS, TV, AND THE INTERNET

CAUTION

Movies, TV, Radio, and Internet materials are not exempt from copyright law. Be sure to stay within the regulations.

Films, TV, radio programs, music, and the Internet are great ways to deepen the impact of your message. The caveat with these types of materials is that

they can be easily misused in the classroom. We've all sat through classes
where the teachers tossed on a movie and sat in the back of the room. More
recently, we witnessed instructors waste time by surfing the Internet during
class in search of relevant examples to show students. Unfortunately, students are used to faculty substituting media for in-depth engagement. Take
care to make your use of media meaningful to avoid turning students off
every time you turn on the monitor or projector.

> **INFO**
>
> **This website includes helpful techniques for accessing videos
> and searching television programs:**
>
> http://www.ciconline.org/thinkingcritically

Picking class materials doesn't need to be overwhelming. You don't have
to have every single reading picked out, or all of your movies and Internet
pages nailed down. If you start planning early enough, previewing can actually be fun. Start with a vision of what materials you think would make for
an interesting and meaningful class. Try to include a manageable variety
of readings, activities, and other media. Find the materials that you like
best and give them a shot. Be creative and don't fear testing out new ideas.
If a book, movie, or any other assignment doesn't work, you can always
change it for next term. Finally, being conscious of the little details (e.g.,
time frames, reading levels, and cost to students) will help you save time by
ruling out inappropriate material.

TO DO LIST

1. Find out how many days/weeks your class spans.
2. Gauge the workload you can reasonably expect of your students.
3. Gauge the reading or comprehension level of your materials.
4. Start previewing your materials at least one month before you have to
   place an order.
5. Select materials that you can reasonably expect students to master in
   the time allotted.
6. Order your materials.
7. Develop a course packet, post articles online, or reserve materials at
   the library. Be sure these are within the bounds of copyright law.
8. Check bookstore and library to make sure your orders are accurate.

3

Pick Your Plan

Syllabi 101

Now that you have figured out your teaching philosophy and what materials you want to use, it's time to develop the rest of the course and fine-tune your ideas. The best way to do this is to design a good syllabus. At this point, you have seen dozens of syllabi throughout your academic career. Think of what made certain syllabi useful and others less so. From a student's perspective, what were some features of the better syllabi that stand out in your mind? If you have never created a syllabus, it should be easy to find good models. Teachers regularly post their syllabi on the Internet (a recent search for "anthropology syllabus" resulted in over one million hits!). Another effective way of gathering examples is to ask your colleagues for copies of their syllabi. This can be especially helpful if you can find a syllabus for the same course that you are teaching. While the content of the sample syllabi might not be similar to your course, the overall outlines will share the same characteristics we describe here.

In examining the samples, take a look at the layout and readability from a student's point of view. How specific is the syllabus in letting students know what is due when? Does important material stand out, or is it buried in a paragraph? As a stranger picking up this syllabus, how well can you guess what goes on in the class? Once you find a public domain sample that works for you, paste it into a word processing document for use as a predesigned template. You can modify this general outline according to your specific needs.

Most high school syllabi tend to be less detailed than those used in college courses, but secondary teachers should not be afraid to include as much information as possible. A thorough syllabus not only helps establish policies and procedures for your particular class, it acts as a guide for both

you and your students. At the college level, we encourage you to think of
your syllabus as a contract between you and your students. It should contain all of the necessary information that a student needs to know about
the course. Leaving out significant points might confuse students or allow
them to dispute your grades and class policies. Below, we list some general
issues to cover.

COURSE INFORMATION

On most syllabi, the first section provides the basic description of the
course and the instructor's contact information. Remember that students
will use all of this information to contact you, so be careful not to mention
any personal information that you don't want publicized. An example of
the course information section might look like this:

Title:	Introduction to Communications
Catalogue #:	COMM 101
Room:	Auditorium 260
Days and Time:	M W F 10:00am–11:00am
Instructor:	Professor Know-it-all
Office Phone #:	555-555-1212
Email:	knowitall@bigstateu.edu
Office Hours:	M W 12:00pm–2:00pm
Office Location:	Rm 248, Office Bldg.

This straightforward listing isn't the most aesthetically pleasing layout, but
it has all the necessary information. If you have a teaching assistant, you
should include his or her name, email, and phone here as well. For high
school teachers, including your room number, email address, and school
phone extension should be adequate.

CLASS DESCRIPTION AND OBJECTIVE

This section goes by many names (such as course overview, description, introduction, or outline). Regardless of the name, this is your opportunity to
communicate to your students what you expect from them. Some schools
require that this section repeat verbatim the course's description in the
course catalogue. Hopefully, you'll have the flexibility to write a description
in a friendly, inviting style such that the students buy into the philosophy
of the class.

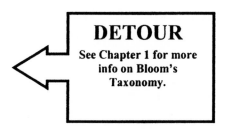

DETOUR

**See Chapter 1 for more
info on Bloom's
Taxonomy.**

One of the first points to mention in your description is any prerequisites or background experience students might need to successfully complete the course. Next, you should state your goals for the class. This lets the students know as specifically as possible what they are expected to have learned by a certain point in time. A good way to develop your course goals is to think of them in terms of "learning outcomes." Step back and ask yourself "Why am I teaching X topic?" or "What do I want them to get out of this course?"

Learning outcomes include specific knowledge or skills students will need to demonstrate. Learning outcomes are *measurable*. You should be able to document student achievement of these outcomes through course activities, assessments, or interviews. While there are many options here, a basic way to phrase such goals and objectives includes a statement phrased along the lines of "Students will be able to . . . " For example:

- Students will be able to apply a Marxist approach to describe education systems in the United States and Latin America.
- Students will be able to use algebraic expressions to explain the basic supply and demand requirements of a small business.
- Students will be able to describe past events in Spanish.
- Students will be able to analyze a text in the creation of a five-page paper.

Alongside these objectives, it makes sense to explain the format of your class. Overall, how will these goals and objectives be achieved? Tell students whether you plan on using a lecture format, seminar structure, cooperative group approach, student-led discussions, or a combination of all of these. Include a description of both your teaching strategies as well as the students' expected participation. They should know if their role will be one of a quiet listener, active discussant, presenter, group member, or something else.

A final point to mention in your course description is the amount of time you expect students to dedicate to your class. This is best phrased as hours per week. Clearly stating such should lessen any complaints about the workload. There are many ways to estimate how much time your students should spend on homework. Advanced high school students usually average half an hour of homework per academic subject per day for a total of two hours of daily homework. Full-time college students can be expected to put in a forty-hour work week, including class hours. You could ask students carrying five classes to complete approximately five hours of homework per week (an amount you might adjust depending on how many credits the class is worth).

Spelling out this time requirement for your students helps them understand what you expect and helps them in juggling their busy schedule. The exercise also helps you define the parameters of your class. As you grow in experience, you'll figure out how much you can reasonably expect of students in your institution and adjust your homework accordingly.

REQUIRED MATERIALS

Following the course description, note the required materials for the class. In addition to listing the materials, direct students to the place where they can purchase or access the materials. We recommend listing the reading materials individually, in a bibliographic format that students can use as an example for any term paper you might assign. If you have a reading packet for the class, you can list it here as well. For example:

- CHEM 481 Reading Packet (available at the Campus Copy Shop)
- Furry, Jarusch. *Bonne Continuation*. New York: Prentice Hall, 2001.
- Errington, J. 2003. "Getting Language Rights: The Rhetorics of Language Endangerment and Loss." *American Anthropologist*. 105(4): 723-732. (Located on Blackboard in Course Documents.)
- Lisa McGirr, "The Passion of Sacco and Vanzetti: A Global History," *The Journal of American History*, March 2007: http://www.history cooperative.org/cgi-bin/justtop.cgi?act (Located on the Library Reserve website.)

List any other materials you require—software, tools, lab supplies and office supplies—in a separate category to avoid confusion.

EVALUATION

A detailed description of your evaluation criteria might be the most crucial part of your syllabus. You can bet that it will be the first section to which the students turn. The more specific you can be about your grading, the better. Students want to know exactly where to aim their efforts and, once grades are assigned, exactly where they fell short. Describe the different means of assessment that you will use (e.g., quizzes, tests, presentations, and homework). An overall breakdown of the grading gives the students a picture how the assignments are weighted. For example:

Midterm Exam:	100pts.	(20%)
Final Exam:	100pts.	(20%)
Homework:	100pts.	(20%)
Research Paper:	100pts.	(20%)
Participation:	100pts.	(20%)
Total:	500pts.	(100%)

If you want to be more detailed, you can break down the points and show them exactly how many they need to earn an A, B, C, D, or F. For example:

Course Requirements

Final Paper	100
Two exams of twenty-five questions each	100
Six quizzes of five questions each	150
Four paragraphs reporting independent research	20
Video and questionnaire	5
Syllabus quiz	10
Small group introduction and response	10
Total possible points	**395**

Grades

A+	=	375–395 points
A	=	355–374 points
A-	=	345–354 points
B+	=	335–344 points
B	=	315–334 points
B-	=	305–314 points
C	=	270–304 points
D	=	230–269 points

Because many instructors are unsatisfied with the lack of nuance that grades convey, they often include statements about what exactly an A, B, or C means. Here, teachers focus on the difference between the above average work indicated by a B and the excellent work indicated by an A. For example,

"An A student demonstrates exceptional knowledge of the topic, always delivers assignments on time, and is never late or absent from class." "Students who earn a B demonstrate above average knowledge of the topic, always deliver assignments on time, and are rarely late or absent from class."

INFO

Grade inflation has most college students and professors viewing 'B' as average. Check out this site for some background on grade inflation:

http:/www.gradeinflation.com/

Another way of communicating grades to your students is to give them an idea of what each grade means in terms of learning according to your teaching philosophy:

D = You understand the material when you see it.
C = You understand the material when you don't see it; you can memorize and regurgitate.
B = You can make connections across bodies of material.
A = You can say something new about these connections.

Notice how each level requires command of the previous levels. Based on Bloom's Taxonomy, this type of outline really gives the students something to think about while working on assignments and contributing to class discussions. However you choose to explain your grades, by doing so on your syllabus, you have a format for working with students who contest the grades they receive. You can ask students to describe how their work qualifies as an A, B, or C as defined in your syllabus.

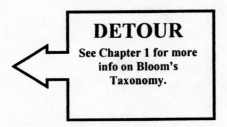

DETOUR
See Chapter 1 for more info on Bloom's Taxonomy.

Should college teachers assign *Incompletes* to students? Be aware that offering students Incompletes can turn out worse for the students than dropping the class or even assigning a failing grade (which, at some schools, can be replaced by retaking the class). While an occasional student does have a situation that deserves an Incomplete (e.g., a severe accident or illness that causes them to miss the final exam or paper), a good portion of students frequently forget to do the makeup work or have a difficult time following through with the paperwork. Consider whether you think the student in question has the independent initiative to finish the work and assign Incompletes sparingly.

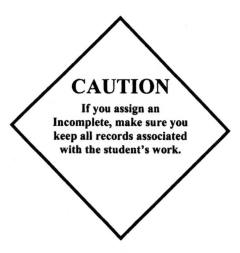

CAUTION

If you assign an Incomplete, make sure you keep all records associated with the student's work.

After you have outlined the overall grading, you might want to describe each assessment in detail. Discussing the exams will give students an idea of what you expect them to know. Since many students suffer from test anxiety, knowing the format of the tests can help calm their nerves. For example:

> Both exams are comprehensive. For the midterm exam, you will be responsible for all of the material covered in the readings and lectures from the beginning of class to the test. For the final exam, you will be responsible for everything covered from the midterm to the end of class. Both tests will include a combination of multiple-choice questions, definitions, short answer, and long answer. Test reviews will be handed out with examples of each type of question.

A brief description of the homework might not seem necessary, but you can explain exactly how you want students to undertake the work, including the format of the product to be assessed. You can also state how you will grade their homework. For example:

> You will complete five homework assignments worth twenty points each. The due dates of each assignment can be found on the course calendar. You are

required to provide a heading that includes your name, the name of the class, the page numbers completed, and the date. You will earn five points for each correct answer; points will be deducted for wrong answers, spelling mistakes, and lack of thoroughness.

Teachers often spend the least amount of time specifying the class participation aspect of students' grades. However, as with other parts of the course grade, the clearer your expectations, the easier it is for students to plot their way toward excellence. Here's an example of a statement on participation:

> This course involves a good amount of participation through both speaking and listening. One of the primary goals of this class is to teach you how to engage in intellectual discussions. While you may not agree with my opinions or those of your classmates, it is expected that you will contribute your own views in a manner that is acceptable in an academic forum. It is important to understand that learning is achieved through the congenial negotiation of ideas. You will be evaluated on how well you contribute to both small and large group discussions, your frequency of participation, and your ability to work with a variety of individuals.

In an even more specific evaluation of participation, we've seen professors use a daily rubric whose categories designate certain kinds of participation, such as "connects discussion to text" and "acknowledges and responds to another student's contribution."

For larger projects such as research papers, the evaluation portion of your syllabus is a nice spot to list your requirements alongside some sort of grading rubric. If you have a preferred paper format or style, specify the details in your syllabus. You can also give students hints on citations, grammar, and other points of writing.

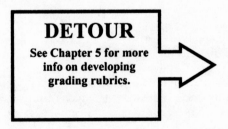

DETOUR
See Chapter 5 for more info on developing grading rubrics.

As you can see, the evaluation portion of your syllabus can be quite lengthy. Stretched for time, you may want to hold off on explaining certain grades—such as papers—until a later point. If this is the case for you, we suggest you include that information in the syllabus the next time you teach the class. Again, the idea here is to give students time to plan, to establish certain expectations for the class, and to allow students to assess during the first days of the course whether your class is a good fit for them.

ATTENDANCE, WITHDRAWALS, AND
MISSED ASSIGNMENTS

While some instructors include the students' attendance in their overall grade, others do not even track it. At the high school level, school districts have policies on how many days a student is allowed to miss before being withdrawn, and you should take into account absences for this and for grading purposes. In a large university class (eighty-some students), keeping accurate attendance records is probably unrealistic (although new electronic response pads or "clickers" are making this easier). In smaller classes, especially those under forty students, you can effectively use attendance as an assessment tool by combining it with participation, perhaps by giving an allotted number of points for each day the student is present. However you choose to deal with attendance, you need to emphasize that student attendance is crucial for their academic development. Then you need to decide whether students will be penalized for not attending and what system of penalties you can realistically enforce.

You'll want to make this decision carefully. Students will regularly test your attendance policy with both legitimate (e.g., illness, car breakdown, family emergency, or work) and illegitimate excuses (e.g., extended holiday weekend or didn't know your attendance policy). It's a rare instructor who relishes talking with a student about absences. Make sure whatever policy you develop is something you can stick to even in uncomfortable circumstances.

CAUTION

Students are good at playing on your soft side, so be wary of creative excuses.

If you decide student absences will affect their grade, explain how in your syllabus. For a college course, you might state something like:

> You are allowed two absences (no questions asked). On your third absence, your final grade will be lowered by five percent; on your fourth absence, your

final grade will be lowered by ten percent; you will be dropped from the course on your fifth absence.

In a college or university setting, the number of times you allow a student to miss will depend on how many credits the course is worth, how often the class meets, and the length of the term.

At the high school level, school, district, and/or state regulations outline how many excused and unexcused absences each student is allowed. Regardless of the official school attendance policy, you should mention how a student's absences will affect her or his grade. For example:

> You will be responsible for making up all work, tests, and assignments missed during an excused absence. Makeup work must be turned in within one week of the absence. Later submissions will not be accepted. For each unexcused absence, you will be penalized five percent of your overall grade. Graded assignments missed during unexcused absences will not be accepted.

Undoubtedly, there will be exceptions due to personal hardship or other uncontrollable factors. You should mention that students need to contact you in such cases. At the same time, if you establish a hard and fast rule, say a cut off at five absences, and a student approaches you on absence number six with a valid excuse due to personal hardship, you are well within your professional boundaries to remind them that your policy already takes their situation into account. You allow five absences for emergencies. If the student hadn't missed the five previous classes, she or he would still have plenty of days to devote to their current situation.

Also, you should point out your policy on withdrawing or dropping students due to absences and other circumstances. Tuition payment issues, financial aid policies, and departmental requirements can make the timeliness of withdrawing a student a crucial issue. If it is the students' responsibility to initiate a withdrawal, they need to be familiar with the proper dates and paperwork for completing this process. If it is your responsibility, then you must know the last date of a student's attendance and the last date for permitted withdrawal. Listing such dates on the syllabus can help both you and your students make a timely and appropriate decision.

Absences inevitably mean students fall out of the class flow, missing assignments, exams, and critical information for which they'll be graded. On your syllabus, you need to state both the students' responsibility for missed work and how you deal with missed exams. Some instructors refuse to accept anything late, while others have a system for deducting points for each day an assignment is overdue. You may opt to tell students that they cannot miss any scheduled tests. But, if they know that they are going to be unavailable on a specific day, you might allow them to take the test early (if they inform you in a timely way).

DISCIPLINARY ACTIONS

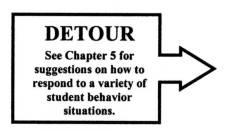

DETOUR
See Chapter 5 for suggestions on how to respond to a variety of student behavior situations.

High school teachers inevitably face behavior problems with their students, and college instructors often have to deal with the same. In most cases, teachers are worried about cheating or plagiarism. Increasingly, schools are requiring teachers include in their syllabi a reference to school policy on this kind of misbehavior. School policies are the first place you should look in writing this section of your syllabus. You'll want to know that whatever consequence you create for students acting in a dishonest or unruly way is supported by your institution. Otherwise, make general mention of what counts as dishonest or inappropriate behavior in class. Note possible consequences to these actions but don't be too concrete. Should a situation arise, you'll want flexibility in choosing your response. Here's some sample language:

> Any form of dishonesty, cheating, plagiarism, sexual harassment, disrespectful, or harmful behavior is a violation of state statutes and university regulations. If demonstrated, such behavior may result in failing the course and/or expulsion from the university. Please refer to the university catalogue for official procedures.

COURSE SCHEDULE

Perhaps the most useful part of the syllabus, for you as well as your students, is a well-designed course schedule. Depending on how specific you want to be, you can outline your calendar according to months, weeks, or days. The most effective way is to state exactly what you expect the students to have completed for each day. The three basic components that students should know for each day that you meet include:

1. what topics you will cover that day;
2. what the students need to have read or prepared for that day;
3. what the students need to hand in on that specific day.

As long as the students can see exactly what is expected of them, the format is up to you. Try to make your calendar so explicit that you aren't flooded with questions like: "Are we supposed to read this chapter for today, or is does it mean to read it for next class?" Some calendars have specific columns for each day:

Table 3.1.   Sample Course Schedule

Date	Topic	Today's Readings	Due
9/15/07	British Colonies	Perkins Ch. 1-4	2-pg. reading summary
9/17/07	British Colonies	Perkins Ch. 5-6	Quiz: British Colonies

Other schedules might just list the day's objectives:

2/15:   Gender and Style in Discourse:

- Read for today: Limon- *Carne, Carnales, and the Carnivalesque: Bakhtinian Batos, Disorder, and Discourse* (Brenneis and Macauly Ch. 10)
- Turn in today: book review #2

2/17:   Cultural Interpretation:

- Read for today: Shaul and Furbee Ch. 10
- Read for today: Cameron- *Performing Gender Identity: Young Men's Talk and the Construction of Heterosexual Masculinity* (handout)

Regardless of your format, having a detailed schedule will help you prepare for upcoming weeks. When designing your course schedule, remember to take special events into consideration, such as conference travel dates and holidays. In fact, one way to plan out your course is to reproduce a monthly calendar in your syllabus. In addition to being able to quickly find special dates, this will give you a visual layout so that you can calculate the amount of work due for each class.

In other words, if your class meets just twice a week, on Tuesdays and Thursdays, you won't want to assign a long reading for Thursday since the students will have just one day to do their homework. Instead, assign the bulk of homework for completion over the weekend. Also, if you are requiring a lengthy project, giving them time during a holiday to advance their work might be a good idea.

At the high school level, you will want to do much the same. A calendar outlay of your objectives and plans for a month is invaluable. Many districts are now requiring their teachers follow or create their own calendar-based approach, something called a Curriculum Map. The Map includes essential questions, content, skills, materials, and assessments.

DISCLAIMER

Finally, include a disclaimer on your syllabus in case something happens and you are forced to change plans. This will prevent students who have missed announcements of changes in class from challenging you on your requirements. Such a statement can be as basic as:

> This syllabus is intended as a guide only. Requirements, class presentations, and assignments may change as circumstances warrant. It is the student's responsibility to inquire about any changes that have been made.

TYING EVERYTHING TOGETHER

REST STOP

Be sure to submit a copy of your syllabi to your department chair or a faculty mentor. Having your syllabus on record communicates to your colleagues exactly what you are doing in classes.

As long as you take into consideration the suggestions we have made here, there is no right or wrong format or length for your syllabus. Some syllabi only take up one or two pages, while others run to fifteen pages. Producing an in-depth syllabus can diminish students' concerns about the course. But, if you decide (or only have time) to give your students a bare bones list be sure to include the most necessary points—how they can contact you and what course materials they need to acquire.

Regardless of how long your syllabus is, take the first day of class to review the document with your students. You might want to have a syllabus quiz prepared for them on the second or third class meeting. This can be a simple take-home or in-class "open note" type of quiz, just as long as it requires students review the syllabus thoroughly. Such a quiz should highlight the most important points of your syllabus. The quiz can also be used to demonstrate that students read the syllabus in case they later have complaints about the rules.

There are a few general concerns that we still need to mention. First, be aware that no matter how thorough your syllabus is, you may still have a student who tries to negotiate every last detail of your course policies. If you encounter such a student, simply say: "In the interest of fairness, I cannot

> ## INFO
>
> **Interested in seeing a model syllabus quiz? Check out our website link for Chapter 3 examples:**
> *Sample Syllabus Quiz.*

change the syllabus for one student." At the same time, a mid-term course evaluation will alert you to any general disgruntlement and allow you to adjust your syllabus to students' needs. Also, consider that your students might not read the syllabus. When students ask you questions about the class—due dates and policies—don't tell them the answer, simply instruct them to look at the syllabus. This is a way of teaching them to be more organized, as well as training them to look at the syllabus before posing questions you've already answered. Make your syllabus accessible to the students by providing a copy online as well as in paper format. This way the students will always have access to the course guide. You should have someone proofread your syllabus before handing it out. Typographical and other errors might dampen student respect for you.

DETOUR

See Chapter 5 for more info on Classroom Assessment Techniques.

If things don't go the way you planned, or even if they go better than planned, keep notes on a master syllabus. Besides scheduling issues, be sure to record what other concerns arise during the semester (e.g., attendance, grades, or workload). After each day, week, section, chapter, jot down your thoughts so that preparing for the next time you teach the class will be that much easier!

> ## INFO
>
> **For multiple examples of syllabus formats, please see our website link for Chapter 3:**
> *Course Syllabi*

Our final, final suggestion for creating the ideal syllabus is for you to remember what even the most well-organized and thorough syllabus doesn't tell you:

- what to do in the classroom;
- how to communicate with your students;
- how to troubleshoot problems;
- how to organize your other professional duties.

The syllabus is a kind of scaffolding from which these other issues hang. Recognizing this distinction early on will help you prepare yourself for the other demands of an academic position. Still, the more explicit and substantive you make your syllabus, the easier it will be to focus on these other issues. You will know your syllabus is a success if throughout the semester you don't get flooded with questions about the class format.

TO DO LIST

1. Find a good model syllabus.
2. Write down all important dates on a calendar.
3. Create a draft of your syllabus.
4. Revise and have someone proofread.

4

Getting on Stage

Delivering a Lesson 101

Now that you have selected your materials, designed your syllabus, and thought about some philosophical approaches to teaching, it is time to perform. The goal of this chapter is to provide you teaching methodologies, strategies, and tricks that will help make your classes more interesting and enjoyable for both you and your students. Good teaching involves many factors: teaching styles, personalities, class size, course content, accessibility of resources, physical layout of classroom, and time. In the following pages, we want to give you an assortment of ideas you can adapt to your personal situation.

LESSON PLANS

The best strategy to ensure that your class flows well is to have a thorough lesson plan, a script of what will happen when and for how long during the course of a single class session. Lesson plans are especially crucial in the early part of a semester, as you set a tone for your course, combine rapport building activities with information delivery, and establish a pattern you expect students to follow.

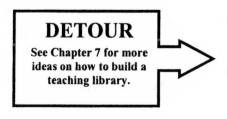

DETOUR

See Chapter 7 for more ideas on how to build a teaching library.

Lesson plans come in many forms, and depending upon your comfort level, they can include word for word what you will say to students. Good lesson plans act as a kind of daily journal for you so that the next time you offer the course you can see day by day how you carried out the class. Organize your plans neatly in a durable binder that can travel with you if necessary. If you don't get through your plan by the end of class, or if an activity takes more or less time than you anticipated, make a note of this so the timing won't slip you up next time you offer the course.

What else should your lesson plan look like? The top of each page should include the calendar date and the number of the course day, that is, where in the class sequence the particular lesson falls. For example, "9/30/06, Day 8," or "September 30, 2006, Day 8 of 30." This way when you look back at your lesson plan, you see not only what date it was on a calendar, but how this lesson fit within the class's overall structure. Later, these plans can be modified to fit another time schedule.

INFO

For examples of lesson plan templates, visit our website link for Chapter 4:
Lesson Plans.

As for what to write in your lesson plan, this depends on how thorough you want to be or the requirements of your school. Using a basic outline like this can be helpful at the college level:

I.   Intro
II. Activity/Topic 1
II. Activity/Topic 2
III. Activity/Topic 3
IV. Close

An introductory section can be used to mention any announcements, remind you to return student assignments, preview the day's lesson, or remind students of where they left things off at the end of the previous class. Under the activity/topic headings, you might want to have explicit instructions on what to discuss, how to arrange the room for an activity, the time allotted for each activity, or even your lecture notes. The closing section is a nice place to list a few points to recap the day's lesson and offer a preview of the next class. If an outline seems too formal, you can make a list of bulleted topics that you want to cover:

- Restaurant Vocabulary in Spanish
  1. main dishes
  2. drinks
  3. desserts
  4. verbs for ordering
  5. verbs for paying

Take a minute to create a template on your computer of your preferred lesson plan style. Then, all you have to do is fill in the blank either before or after class, again, as specifically as possible.

At the high school level, you may find your program has a preferred format. Ask your department chair or a school administrator. If there is no preferred format, then we suggest the following:

- Identify the state educational standards which will be addressed.
- Identify your objectives (what you want the students to learn).
- List the materials you'll need, and materials students will need.
- Outline the design of the lesson, the step-by-step procedures.
- State any adaptations in the lesson for learning-disabled or gifted students.
- Describe the assessment that will be used.

Beginning teachers at any level benefit from erring on the side of including more detail in your lesson plans. Remember, you'll be returning to your lesson plans the next time you teach the class. You might think you'll remember all the details, but a lot can happen between course offerings. A vague lesson plan will leave you questioning, "What does 'discuss topic A' mean? How did we do that?"

Regardless of how you structure your lesson plan, it's a good idea to write out a few questions you anticipate students will pose. By including the answers to these questions in your lesson plan, you won't have to come up with ideas on the spot. If you make overhead transparencies of your lesson plan, write it on the board, or post it online, your plan becomes an outline that keeps both you and your students on track. Your lesson plan can work extra hard if you share it with students who missed class.

If you don't have time to make a lesson plan every class session, at least keep notes of what you covered in class so that you can remain organized as the semester progresses. Now that we have mentioned some basic points on preparing for class, we want to outline some methods to use during the class itself.

LECTURES

It's interesting that one of the most common teaching methods is, increasingly, one of the most controversial. Lectures gain a bad reputation when used poorly—when the instructor stands in front of the class, maybe behind a podium, and talks for forty-five minutes without a break. However, implemented correctly, the lecture can be a powerful tool. In comparison to the other styles, lectures allow instructors to convey a large amount of information. Some colleges are finding that large lecture halls are the classes alumni remember most about their college experience. The trick to good lecturing is to create a lecture environment that assures students learn and retain all that information.

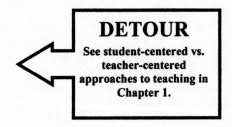

DETOUR

See student-centered vs. teacher-centered approaches to teaching in Chapter 1.

Here are a few ideas aimed at helping student learning in a lecture class. The suggestions share one common theme. They each help students break up the lecture into manageable chunks. For example, you might offer students some sort of graphic organizer of your lecture. This may be an outline, a flow chart, or a copy of your PowerPoint slides. Students then use the organizer to take notes and participate in the lecture as active listeners. The organizer should be bare bones—just enough so students can keep up with you. It shouldn't be so specific that students know where the lecture is headed. If you hand out a detailed outline, students may read this in the first few minutes and spend the rest of the class period impatient for the inevitable conclusion.

REST STOP

When planning out your lesson, make sure that the activities are calculated for students to shift from passive knowledge recipient to active learner. Have them:

- actively participate;
- connect ideas from other class sessions or courses;
- explain difficult concepts in their own words.

Another strategy entails breaking up your lectures into segments of ten or fifteen minutes, leaving time in between for other activities or discussions. For example, you can start off a class session by posing questions about the previous lecture or readings. Give students a few minutes to discuss their thoughts with a partner or jot down a response. Then call on a few students for answers. Use the questions and responses to bridge into your lecture for the current day. After lecturing for a short time period, have everyone write down something about your lecture that was unclear, left them confused, or something that was a new piece of knowledge. Call on a few students (or ask for volunteers) and expand on their comments. Finally, use those comments as a bridge to your next lecture segment.

Other short activities include showing movie clips or slides, having students write a one- or two-minute paper, and having students do short three- to five-minute presentations between lecture segments. In a one-hour class, you can fit two solid lecture sessions with time in the middle for an applied activity like a small group discussion or worksheet.

Another way to spice up a lecture is to bring in some visual aids. This can include anything from photographs, charts, maps, food, toys, artifacts, to guest lecturers. Visual aids make the course material more interesting and meaningful for everyone (especially visual and tactile learners). If possible, pass your visual aids around for the students to hold and inspect on a closer level. You can even ask students to bring in visual aids and have them present on their significance to the class material. After talking about an object or image, give the students a chance to ask questions or describe it in their own words.

Regardless of how you structure your lecture, take extra care with the information you know will only be available to students through the lecture. This information is an especially good candidate for further consideration in class activities. Flag the information as deserving students' close attention and make sure the tempo of your lecture allows students to take detailed notes. Pause at the end of this lecture section for questions. Perhaps have students read back to you their notes or create a visual of their own to complement the notes. As with other parts of your lecturing, approach this material strategically and ask yourself both how well you've conveyed the information and what steps you have taken to aid learning and retention.

REST STOP

Don't be afraid to repeat information from previous lectures. Weaving prior information into new material helps students understand how different concepts are related on a bigger scale.

COOPERATIVE GROUPS

Establishing an effective cooperative-group format is one of the best ways to get your students actively involved in the learning process. Usually, cooperative-group activities consist of students working in groups of two to five people. By preparing specific activities that call for participation and cooperation, you can ensure that all of your students are given the opportunity to actively use what they have learned. Following a few basic steps will enable you to create a constructive and nurturing environment that endures.

> ## INFO
>
> **If you'd like more background info on cooperative groups, stop by our website or visit:**
>
> www.atozteacherstuff.com/pages/1875.shtml

The first step in applying a cooperative-group system is organizing the layout of the classroom. We recommend that you move the desks or tables in the room such that the groups are neatly arranged and everyone in the group can see you and the board without having to turn around or crane their necks. You might have to take a few minutes before class to arrange the desks in the way you want them, but after a few class sessions, the students will be used to your system and know how to arrange their own groups. If possible, have your students sit like this at all times, even if you are lecturing. Having them sit in groups on a daily basis makes students feel more comfortable when you begin an activity, and it avoids wasting time moving chairs. In lecture halls, the room constraints can make this difficult. In this case, you can have the students form clusters with the other students closest to them. Even in an auditorium-style class, you can have people work with those sitting next to and behind them.

> # REST STOP
>
> Take some time before the semester to visit your classrooms. Plan out how you want to organize your groups. Move the desks or tables around into groups. Try sitting in a few of the groups to make sure everyone will have a good view of you. Sketch out the best seating arrangement so you will have it ready to go on the first day!

After figuring out the seating arrangement for your classroom, you'll need to prepare a few strategies for assigning students to groups. Allowing students to sit wherever they choose is fine, especially during the first few days of the semester. Unless you want your students sitting with the same people every time, you need to come up with a way to get them to mingle. You can do this by changing their seats once a week, chapter, or month (this is good for placing students with different types of intelligences together). Students might sign up for groups based on their common interest in a topic that will form part of the group's work.

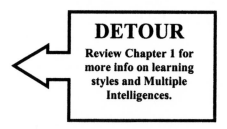

DETOUR

Review Chapter 1 for more info on learning styles and Multiple Intelligences.

One way to randomly place students in groups is to figure what size group you want (e.g., 4) and divide the number of total students (e.g., 28) by that number (e.g., 28/4 = 7). Then count off the students by, in this case seven, and assign each number to a group of desks or tables, such that all the 1s are together, 2s are together, etc. If there is an odd number, simply have one odd-sized group. Another way is to have students draw from a lottery when they first come to class and then direct them to the predetermined group according to what they have drawn (colored candy works well for this). Be creative, just try and get the students to work with a variety of partners throughout the course. Grouping the students might be a little chaotic the first few times, but they will get used to it and waste less time as the semester goes on.

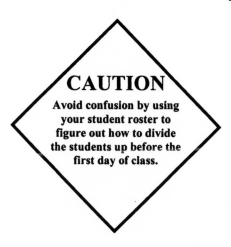

CAUTION

Avoid confusion by using your student roster to figure out how to divide the students up before the first day of class.

Once you have scouted out the classroom and designed a good seating system, you are ready to start planning group-oriented activities. One
common mistake made by teachers at all levels is expecting students to
automatically participate in groups. If you want your students to work in
groups, it is important that you give them a chance to get to know each
other first. First, establish some basic rules for working in groups (especially
at the beginning of the term). Rules could include:

- everyone's opinion counts;
- everyone gets an opportunity to speak or participate;
- listen at least twice as much as you speak;
- if you don't agree with someone, you should acknowledge the disagreement in a positive way;
- chit-chat is fine once you have completed your task.

Next, incorporate some basic team-building activities into your lessons.
Team-building activities include any type of task that requires students to
work together in a low-stress environment so that they become accustomed
to operating as a group.

You should implement team-building activities during the first few class
sessions.

INFO

**Check out these sites for more ideas on classroom icebreakers
and community building:**

www.education-world.com/a_lesson/lesson/lesson131.shtml
www.eslflow.com/ICEBREAKERSreal.html

One example of team-building includes assigning debate topics and di-
viding the group members into pro and con sides. In a group of four, assign
the two students on the right to argue in favor of an issue, and the two on
the left to argue against it. Get them comfortable debating by assigning a
frivolous topic (e.g., football vs. baseball; coffee—good or bad). Tell them
that they can only speak for thirty seconds or a minute at a time, and they
have to alternate turns. Also, tell students that before they can state their
opinion, they must first recap what their opponent just said. You can give
them whatever suggestions or rules you think ensure a good, amiable discussion.

Now that you have students accustomed to working together, you'll want
to ensure participation by everyone in the group. You can accomplish this
by appointing someone to start a task and then indicate the order in which

others should follow. Tell them to go from shortest to tallest, in order of age, by lightest to darkest color pants, clockwise, or whatever other oddity comes to you.

A number system is an efficient means of fostering your students' participation. In a group of four, assign the students numbers within the group such that each student is person #1, #2, #3, or #4. In any given activity, you can have person 1 be responsible for question Z, person 2 for question X, person 3 for Y, and person 4 for W. One person might record the conversation, another act as time keeper for the activity, while another is the group's public spokesperson. A number system is also good because you can have students work in small groups, then bring them together in new combinations to continue the activity or teach one another what they learned. This is done easily by assigning the different numbers to different corners. "All 1s go to the back corner. All 2s to the front corner." Once students are grouped by number, each person can act as a representative of their small group, elaborating on their work.

INFO

For some great cooperative learning activities, check out:

http://edtech.kennesaw.edu/intech/cooperativelearning.htm#activities

and

http://www.utc.edu/Administration/WalkerTeachingResourceCenter/FacultyDevelopment/CooperativeLearning/index.html#return

---

Cooperative-group activities force students to pay attention to each other while at the same time ensuring maximum participation from everyone. In cooperative-group activities, students review material repeatedly and absorb it in new ways as they act as both teacher and student. The biggest challenge for the instructor in these activities is to be well prepared. While writing your lesson plans, make sure that you diversify the types of activities you request from one class session to the next. Allot a certain amount of time for each activity and stick to it. You can easily alternate lecture, group activities, and media clips—all within one class session. Remember, a noisy classroom is a sign of an active learning environment!

SEMINAR CLASSES AND GROUP DISCUSSIONS

While seminar classes are usually defined by their small size (ten to twenty students), advanced readings, and class conversation, the following suggestions can also be applied to all other class discussion situations. Seminars and group discussions require subtle structuring to make them more meaningful to students. This structuring includes the physical space as well as the social space.

If possible, you should arrange the room so that everyone can see each other. Some instructors like a more traditional classroom setting from which they can lead the discussions. However, this style can isolate the students from each other, inhibit an interactive atmosphere, and lend itself to a teacher-centered classroom. Instead, under optimal circumstances, students in a seminar class would sit around a big table where no single person is the focus of attention. If a table isn't available, instructors will place the desks in a circle or square, including themselves in the group. Others prefer a semicircle, placing themselves at the top so that everyone is focused on them.

Once you have figured your preferred seating arrangement, you need to develop a method to stimulate lively discussions. The best seminar classes are the ones where students take ownership and feel confident about discussing the material. You can start the ball rolling by having some specific topics or questions. If you begin the class with the question "So, what do you think about the reading?" you'll likely receive blank stares. You might want to begin by having the students sum up some of the main points. After you know that they understand the basics, you can start asking them to give their opinions and apply the concepts in different ways. Be sure the questions you have on hand are broad enough to allow for maximum participation but structured enough so students have something concrete to address.

This questioning process might still have you as the focus of the discussion. Shift the attention away from you and toward students' independent thinking by having them prepare their own discussion questions for class. In a small class, everyone can ask their question to the group. In a larger class, you can split students into pairs or small groups that respond to their questions. Another strategy is for you to develop some questions and have the students discuss them in small groups first, then come back together as a class to explore the different viewpoints.

If you'd like your students to lead a class, you can assign each person to present on a particular reading or topic by creating questions or activities. In our seminar classes, we give the students latitude to structure the class as they wish. We suggest they might take us for a walk or have us stand on our heads! As it turns out, they never have us stand on our heads, but once they know we welcome their experimentation, they come up with creative activities that engage the material on a deeper level.

As in all discussion and seminar formats, the key is for you as the teacher to remain in the background. If you talk too much, students will remain

```
INFO

For a description of seminar participation, see:

http://records.viu.ca/~johnstoi/seminars.htm
```

quiet. Students will speak up once they know you won't fill the quiet. At the beginning of a seminar course, be patient during awkward silences. If, in your mind, you begin to count as soon as you feel uncomfortable, you'll find the silence rarely lasts longer than thirty seconds. At the same time, you can encourage participation by creating a direct connection between student participation and their grade. Use a rubric that allows you to keep track of who speaks up. Try rewarding initial input with chocolate or candy. Compliment students on their insights and make an effort to understand their logic if they don't quite have the language to say what they're thinking. Whatever your strategy, the main objective is to engage the students and have them engage each other.

STUDENT PRESENTATIONS

Usually, presentations come in the form of standing up in front of the class and describing a final project. More often than not, these can be troublesome for the student presenter, especially in front of a large class. A lack of training and the usual public-speaking anxiety may undermine a student's actual knowledge of the material. Instead of learning from the student presenter, your other students might become bored or miss the major points. However, if you prepare your students well enough, these types of activities can be beneficial for everyone. You'll be able to utilize student presentations throughout the course as an instructional tool, while at the same time developing their pubic-speaking skills. Optimally, your students will develop their presentation skills and learn from each other's presentations.

Presentations become easier once you acknowledge that a presentation doesn't have to mean standing in front of the class behind a podium. You can have students "teach" small sections of the material. You can have them develop and lead discussions in a small or large group. Or, students might work in teams to make a presentation that models a television show, a board game, or popular music.

Any way you decide to implement presentations, the most important thing to remember is that (most of the time) you can't expect students to get up in front of their peers and feel relaxed enough to deliver an informative and captivating presentation on their first (or even second) try. Students need to practice their presentations, and you have to model what you consider to be a good presentation for your students. In addition to incorporating practice periods into your classroom, clearly write out for your students your expectations. Ask yourself questions about the quality of the content you expect. Then ask yourself questions about the presentation style itself:

- Do you want your students to read their presentation?
- Should they have some sort of handout or visual aid for their peers?
- How much time do they have?
- What types of media can they use (e.g., overhead, PowerPoint, chalkboard, or poster board), and do they know how to use them correctly?
- Do they know not to turn their back to the class while speaking (and writing on the board)?
- How should they deal with any nervousness?

Another crucial feature of cultivating student presenters is to provide them with critical but encouraging feedback. You can also incorporate the other members of the class in this process to encourage active listening. For every presentation, you can have your students answer some basic questions, such as:

1. What did you learn from this presentation?
2. What is something that you liked about this presentation?
3. What is something that the presenter could improve upon for next time?

You can collect these sheets, read through them, and give them to the presenter during the next class. This way, not only do you see what other students thought about the presentation and give presenters a variety of feedback, you also help students recognize the characteristics (both good and bad) of presenting in front of a group. Be aware that, as with the presentation itself, you should also model these types of critiques so students know how to assess a good presentation. You can do this by analyzing the work of other speakers, such as guest lecturers and famous speakers.

Student presentations work best when they are made meaningful for everyone, not just the presenters. Add depth to presentations by having students incorporate course material into their presentations and by including the presentations in your own discussions, lectures, and even testing materials. If students know the presentations are part of the whole class (i.e., not just part of someone else's grade) and important to their final grade (i.e., part of the final exam), they will be more motivated to take them as a learning opportunity.

EFFECTIVE USE OF EDUCATIONAL TOOLS AND MEDIA

As we mentioned in chapter 2, media and other visual methods can significantly galvanize your students' understanding of the material. From this stance, we strongly encourage you to use a variety of media and other tools in your teaching. Unfortunately, many instructors use the media in ways that leave the students bored or confused. Below, we list a few common types of media, and a few suggestions on how to make them work for you.

- *Movies:* While showing a film in its entirety might be a good idea in some cases, you can make a film even more meaningful by showing clips and designing activities around them. Even a five- to twenty-minute clip can enhance your discussion by giving the students a visual cue. Longer clips are fine too, but try to make the amount of information manageable for an adequate discussion. You can also strategically stop films in certain places so students have to guess what happens or create their own ending.
- *PowerPoint:* More and more, PowerPoint presentations are the main vehicle for classroom lectures. Used correctly, PowerPoint presentations can significantly enhance your classes. Yet, the most common applications are less than captivating. It seems a preferred strategy to write long paragraphs on each slide, and then read this text during class. This might make it easy for the students to copy down what you have on the slide, but it usually takes them so long to write the information that they miss any other commentary you offer. Instead, include short phrases and key words and concepts on your slides. A good rule of thumb is to limit your slides to four lines of five to seven words each. Then talk about the individual slides and field questions as you go. Use the PowerPoint to show pictures, charts, and maps. You can also attach video streams and other stimulating graphics. If you make it interesting enough, your students might want copies of your presentation (you can either email them a copy or make it available online). PowerPoint is most effective as an occasional tool, not an everyday crutch. Used repeatedly, PowerPoint can impose a dull and predictable rhythm to a class.
- *The Internet:* Even though your students have access to the Internet, you can still include it as an effective tool in your classroom. We don't suggest surfing the Net in the middle of class, but if your classroom is equipped with a projection unit, you can bring up appropriate sites or do a quick search for a spontaneously suggested topic. Depending on what you are teaching, you should have time to find one or two websites to demonstrate your material visually. Why spend a lot of time

creating charts, graphs, maps, and other visual aids if they are easily accessible online? A caveat: many professors are concerned about the poor quality of info online. If this matters to you, plot out a search that demonstrates the Web's pitfalls and shows students how to navigate toward quality info. Again, plan your search ahead of time and use the Web for an in-class demonstration.

REST STOP

To avoid getting lost on the Internet during class, save the websites you want to use in your "favorites" file or copy and paste a list of web addresses in an email. Put the links in the order that you want to show them to your students.

- *Music:* If you are studying music, it only makes sense to bring in the actual song for your students to hear. Maybe you are looking at the political messages in pop culture, doing a cross-cultural analysis of metaphors, or even searching for creative features in the lyrics of a song. These are all great opportunities to bring in real music for your students to experience. Even if you aren't studying a piece of music per se, you can still bring in a little radio and play background music during group activities. This is really fun if you can find music that somehow applies to the material or places that you are studying.
- *Guest Speakers:* Bringing in a guest speaker is one of the most powerful and intriguing strategies you can use. You just need to make sure that both your speaker and your students are prepared for each other. You can do this by providing your students with some background reading and questions before the speaker comes to class. It is also a good idea to have your students prepare questions for the speaker based on the readings. You can have them turn the questions in to you either before class (so that you can give the questions to the speaker prior to their delivery), or you can have them direct their questions to your visitor. As for helping out your guest, you can also give your speaker some points that you would like him or her to cover. Make sure that your guest is comfortable during class. Have a comfortable chair for your guest; a bottle of water; a microphone (if necessary); and, if possible, invite your guest to lunch or coffee before the class so she has some time to settle in to the new environment. If your guest has a positive experience, she will more likely return!

- *Discussion Boards, Wikis, Chat Rooms, and Blogs:* One way to provide space for students to express themselves anonymously or by name is to create some type of online discussion board or chat room. Teachers increasingly count online discussion as a continuation of class time. You can even incorporate this as part of their homework. Creating a discussion board, blog, or wiki can usually be done via a school's on-line host (such as Blackboard), on your own professional website, or on any number of personal web-spaces (e.g., myspace.com). Check with your technology support department for help with this. Having a place for students to continue talking outside of class gives them time to think about the material and class events. This is especially beneficial for the quieter students. You can participate as a discussant, moderate and post topics for discussion, use the postings as graded assignments, or review what is being said and tie in the students' posted comments with your next lesson. Online discussion forums are very common outside of the school arena, so playing to students' strengths will only improve your class.

Make sure whatever you convey through media is directly applicable to the material you are covering. Importantly, integrate the media with your other course material so students' attention and motivation remain high. Always have media assignments accompanied by a writing or presentation task. Provide the students with a set of points or questions that they should answer while watching, listening, or surfing. These basic tips can make your classes move along quickly and help your students get the most out of whatever media you choose.

EXTRACURRICULAR STRATEGIES

Sometimes the most effective and meaningful teaching techniques don't take place in the classroom. One way to make your students appreciate your class and the material they are studying is to get them outside of the classroom. One of the best ways to do this is to organize a field trip. Field trips can take many different forms, from an official trip with reservations and transportation to having your class meet up at a given spot. Museums, historical ruins, parks, and community celebrations are all great examples of possible field experiences. In some cases, though, you don't even have to attend the trip, just have students go on their own and report back to you in class. Make sure to announce any community or school events that might be of interest to your students and include these kinds of experiences in your grading. Have students report their experience in the form of writing, such as observations, character sketches, or chronology of events. If you already know what to expect from a particular excursion, you can give students a specific assignment to undertake at the site. For example, you can give them a list of questions or problems to solve that have to do with the place you are visiting. If you want to make it a little more lighthearted, you can create a scavenger-hunt activity or have them interview certain people.

Another good way to get students to experience your topic outside the classroom is to have them form discussion groups of three to six people. As part of their grade, you can have them meet once a week for an hour and discuss the material from class. You can have them either turn in a summary of what they discussed, or even use their thoughts as part of a larger class conversation. This also gives students a chance to vent their frustrations and seek help from each other on difficult assignments. Suggesting that they meet in an online chat room, in a school cafeteria, or bookstore makes the meeting more relaxed, but also shows them that they can carry on those types of conversations in different places.

WEIGHING YOUR OPTIONS

In this chapter, we've covered a lot of different ways of communicating your course material to your students. While applying all of these strategies might be impossible, you can always use a combination of ideas once you get a feel for your students, classroom, and other resources. Regardless of which techniques you try, don't get stuck in a rut. Even if something works for you, be adventurous and try different methods that appeal to you. After a few semesters you will settle into a basic teaching style, from which you can still learn new things. As you experiment, accept critical and constructive feedback from your students. Look for *patterns* in their comments that suggest needed change and recognize helpful suggestions. Ask students to evaluate your class experiments immediately and separately from the course as a whole. This will forestall lingering discomfort for trials gone awry and give you the specific information you need. Remember, the best teachers are good learners themselves!

INFO

We recommend this spot for ideas on how to use student evaluations:
http://www.isu.edu/ctl/facultydev/extras/student-evals.html

TO DO LIST

1. Find out how many students you have per class.
2. Inspect your assigned classroom to see how amenable it is to different seating arrangements.
3. Create a lesson plan template.
4. Write out a lesson plan for each class.
5. Detail in your lesson plan as much as possible how the class will be conducted.
6. Following each class, note in your lesson plan any differences between your intentions and how events worked in practice.
7. Keep your lesson plans and other course materials (syllabus, lecture notes, directions for paper writing, and other activities) in a binder for future reference.

5

Keep It Running Smoothly

Classroom Management and Grading 101

The goal of this chapter is to tap into the knowledge base that most high school teachers have about student conduct and creating a classroom atmosphere conducive to learning. Teachers certified in secondary education undertake observations, internships, and student teaching to learn everything from lesson planning to handling classroom disruptions. Here we learn from them on how to respond to student misbehavior and how to communicate with students in classroom discussions, as well as in graded and non-graded assessments.

CLASSROOM MANAGEMENT:
COUNTERACTING THE NEGATIVES

The phrase "classroom management" usually suggests a strategy for handling problem situations. For our purposes, we extend this concept to include all types of student interactions as well as the overall tone a teacher sets in the classroom. At the college level, you won't have to deal with serious disruptions on a daily basis. Yet, professors do have to deal with incidents that can make teaching difficult. High school teachers have a repertoire of techniques to manage overly talkative, assertive, or sleepy students. By implementing some basic classroom management early on, you can not only stop unwanted behavior (such as loud talking), you can also encourage positive types of interaction (like courteous discussion).

Your first goal is to establish with your students an understanding about when they can talk and when they should listen. This might seem obvious, but how many times have you seen a teacher stand up in front of class ready to talk, only to be trapped behind a wall of student conversations? On the one hand, you want your students to feel comfortable talking to each other so they can benefit from their discussions. On the other, it can be frustrating trying to corral your students' attention. The main technique for catching the students' attention is to start talking loudly or say something like "Okay, it's time to start . . . " or greet your students loudly with a "Good morning, ladies and gentlemen." Verbally getting all students' attention at once is a skill developed over time. With practice, this technique generally suffices but often results in time lost, as students take a moment to settle down.

To avoid wasting time, establish an attention-getting technique on the first day you meet with your students. At the beginning of class, some teachers have an assignment posted, and students know that as soon as they sit in their chair, they need to start working on the assignment. You can create some type of signal for students, so they know when it's time to be quiet and attentive. You might want to use a raised hand to signal quiet. Tell them that if they see you in front of class with your hand raised, it's time to finish their thought and pay attention. Depending on the room, you can flash the lights on and off as a signal. You can walk through the room and tell each group to finish their thought in the next minute, then pay attention up front. Some teachers like to use sound prompts. Counting down from ten allows students time to quickly finish their discussion. If you have a really large class, you can use a small bell or some other noisemaker. Whatever you decide, use your preferred technique consistently and, after a few class periods, students will know exactly when you need them to pay attention.

Even with a great attention-getting technique, you will probably still have instances of unwanted behavior. Here are a few examples of disruptive behaviors and some ways to deal with them:

1. A student continues talking or making noise while you are talking:
   - First, stop talking and look at the student. Usually this is enough to get the student's attention, or at least the attention of people around the student. You can also call on the student to answer a question. Depending on your classroom layout, you can simply continue talking as you walk over and stand next to the student. If the behavior continues, you can ask the student to change seats.

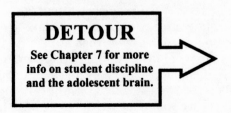

DETOUR
See Chapter 7 for more info on student discipline and the adolescent brain.

2. A student uses foul or abusive language:
   - Don't laugh, even if the obscenity is meant to be a joke or took place in students' private conversation. Address the gaffe immediately. If the obscenity was loud enough for you to hear, you can bet the other students heard it too. Tell the offending student their language is inappropriate. If the remark is overheard by the entire class, address the student in front of everyone. Avoid making a spectacle out of the student, just quietly tell the student those remarks are offensive and disrespectful to the class.
3. A student dominates a discussion and does not let other people talk:
   - Acknowledge the student's enthusiasm and then call on others for their opinions. After class, encourage the student's participation and follow this praise with a request to allow others to contribute. If a student is dominating a small-group discussion, walk over and establish a rule that each person has to say one thing and wait until everyone else has finished before talking again. You can also sit in on the discussion and make it a point to ask the other students questions to give them time to talk. If these techniques fail to resolve the situation, take the student aside and personally request that everyone be allowed to speak before she or he responds.
4. A student habitually arrives late to class:
   - If you are very concerned about students arriving on time, you can always deny them entry after the class has started. You can also create a system that penalizes late arrivals, by including a tardiness clause in your syllabus. Give students a few days to arrive tardy, but tell them that after the second or third tardy, you will subtract five percent from their final grade for each subsequent late arrival. Except in large lecture courses, most students are prompt most of the time, so these measures aren't generally necessary. If you have a case where a particular student arrives late frequently, discuss the situation with her or him. Some students are simply poor schedulers or get trapped in a class, job, or traffic that regularly runs late. Even still, you have the authority to request students arrive on time.
5. Students who leave early, sleep, read the newspaper, or engage in any other non-classroom activities:
   - The best way to handle non-classroom behavior is to address it immediately. This should be carried out in a professional and respectful manner, either in front of the class or individually. If students are reading the newspaper or playing with their cell phones, go ahead and ask them to rejoin class or step outside. Along with embarrassing the student to a certain degree, you are also communicating to the rest of the class that you aren't going to accept such

behavior. As for cell phones, if you allow them in your class at all, require your students place their phones on *silent* mode. Other behavior like sleeping and leaving early can be addressed on a more individual level. If students need to leave early, tell them to inform you before class and have them sit at the back of the room. You can also make early departures count as a tardy or even half-absence. As for sleepy students, we need to remember that they have a lot going on in their lives and falling asleep might not be a direct reflection of you or your class. Walk over and tap the student on the shoulder as you circulate through the class. If you notice sleeping is a recurring habit, you might tell the student to stand up in the back of the room and take notes. If the student does not heed your advice, you can ask the student to go home.

CAUTION

In case of emergency, have the phone number for campus security programmed in your cell phone.

6. A student becomes hostile with you or another student:
   - These cases can be quite serious, so be sure to carefully follow your campus guidelines on hostile students and notify your supervisor, school counselor, and any other relevant authorities if a student acts in a threatening manner. You don't want to minimize the problem, nor do you want to exacerbate it. If an incident arises unexpectedly in class, you'll want to act quickly. First, stop class and ask the student to step outside the room with you. Try to remain calm (even if the student offends you) and state that if the behavior doesn't cease, the student will have to leave the class. If the student personally insults you, immediately request that the student leave your class. If the student objects, call campus security. When class is over, you should report this incident immediately to relevant authorities and seek support for any subsequent interactions with the student.

7. A student is intoxicated or under the influence:
   - In today's world, drugs are an unfortunate fact of some students' lives. Teachers need to take drug use seriously, especially because high schoolers and college students risk lifelong addictions through excessive use. In the immediate present, a student who is physically impaired may pose a danger to the other students. Here, your school polices will be important to determining how you should respond. High school teachers might be required to send a student to the nurse's office. A quick telephone call to the nurse while the child is en route will alert the nurse to your concern. At the college level, if you suspect one of your students is under the influence, pull the student aside and ask if she has taken any type of medication. If the student has a prescription, you can ask if he or she feels well enough to stay in class. If you detect that someone in your class has been using an illicit drug, calmly suggest the student go home and add that she needs to speak with you before the next class hour. Use the intervening time to ask a school counselor for advice on dealing with the situation. (Counselors may have access to psychological information on the student.) Usually, telling students not to come to your class in that state again is enough to resolve the matter. But, you should also let your chairperson know what happened just in case the incident occurs again.
8. A student requests a higher grade:
   - There are two contexts in which this usually occurs. First, it is possible that a student honestly thinks you have made a grading mistake (which is always possible). In this case, sit down with the student and review the test or assignment. If you are confident in your grading, explain why you assigned the grade in question and ask if the student understands your explanation. If the assessment includes subjective responses, offer the student examples of more appropriate or correct answers. The other instance of grade challenges involves "grade grubbing," students who try to convince you to raise their grade without a substantive reason. Grade grubbers usually have grades that are very near the next highest grade. These students can be very persuasive. Remind the student that you have to be consistent in the way you grade all your students. On an individual basis, you can point out specific instances on tests and assignments that have contributed to the student's lower grade. Of course, if you feel that the student is justified, go ahead and adjust the grade accordingly.

Teaching presents constantly changing situations, new personalities, and new situations to navigate. Some of these situations may be challenging. Beginning teachers might be tempted to negotiate with students to ease awk-

CAUTION

**Be aware—once students
learn that you raised one
person's grade, many
others will request the
same.**

ward situations. We suggest you don't enter into negotiations with students. Instead, as in all your conversations with students, speak calmly. The tone you set is crucial to determining whether a disagreement grows into a conflict. Avoid any appearance of accusing a student and, in the briefest language possible, acknowledge the situation ("I understand it's a long walk from Building X to here."), then state your position ("Nonetheless, class policy requires an on-time arrival."). If you think students have a legitimate concern, use your prerogative to change the rules, again, briefly and confidently. ("I recognize that a number of students aren't getting as much opportunity as they might like to contribute to class discussion, so I'll be limiting any one person's talking to two minutes at a stretch.") If you feel a student's actions have caught you off guard, and whenever you feel too put on the spot to make a good decision, the phrase "I will think about this," lets students know that you will return to the matter when you have had time to give it careful consideration.

As you gain experience, handling awkward situations will become second nature and you will create your own vocabulary and stock phrases meant to keep the classroom running smoothly. The best overall method to deal with disturbances is to be consistent and calm, especially as students are getting to know you. Remember, your own fear, anger, or disappointment can undermine your ability to deal effectively with students, but plenty of teachers have faked a cool confidence and effectively turned around awkward situations.

CLASSROOM MANAGEMENT: ENCOURAGING THE POSITIVE

When thinking about encouraging positive behavior, consider how your students approach your class. Their experiences tend to be divided between the day-to-day class workings and the graded assignments. We've already seen how your teaching style creates a daily atmosphere. Here we consider the give-and-take of posing questions to students and engaging in conversation. The kinds and amount of graded assignments affect students' anxiety levels. So, following this section, we talk about how you can add to graded assignments a series of brief, non-graded assessments. Non-graded assessments show you whether students are learning, and they let students know how they fare on material that will appear on tests, quizzes, or papers.

Instructors often rely on spontaneous questioning to spur classroom discussion. Regardless of your teaching style, focusing on your questioning techniques can significantly enhance your classroom management. Questions can create an attentive atmosphere in your classroom, and by being conscious of your questioning patterns and techniques you can deepen students' learning.

Consider a few fundamental characteristics of questioning techniques. Who are you calling on? Why? How often do you call on that student? We have all been in classes where the teacher repeatedly calls on the smartest kid for an easy answer. In other classes, teachers tend to call only on students seated in the front row or students from a certain group. Some teachers, trying to be fair, may call on an equal number of female and male students, although, this still doesn't guarantee broad participation. The same, likely candidates often end up answering questions. You can encourage positive classroom interactions by calling on everyone at least once, periodically, and expanding participation as much as possible. Even students who don't want to speak should be included here. Students who know they will be responsible for answering a question will pay closer attention to classroom activities.

If your class is large, one way to direct questions and comments to students is to establish some kind of rotating pattern. You can divide the class up into four parts. When you pose questions or ask for comments, rotate from section to section, calling on different students each time. If the students are sitting in groups, assign a specific person from each group to be a spokesperson for the group's comments, then rotate spokespeople each class. Some teachers are using computer software to randomly select student participants (see Rest Stop), thereby de-personalizing the process entirely. Or, try placing the names on a deck of cards. Shuffle the cards and call on students according to how they appear in the deck.

Regardless of your system, the point to remember here is that your students will quickly learn your pattern. If students feel like they aren't in your network of answerers, they will become less engaged. If students know that, after a few seconds of silence, you'll jump in with the answer to your own question, they'll play a waiting game. Yes, speaking up in class is frightening for some students, but providing everyone the opportunity to demonstrate their knowledge gives all students help in overcoming their anxieties. When you include as many students as possible in your questioning, the whole class will be more attentive and stay on task.

REST STOP

For very large classes, Excel spreadsheets allow you to randomly select students. First, create a spreadsheet and assign the students to a column, so each has a unique identifying number. Next, click on the Add-Ins portion of the 'Tools' menu, where you should see the 'Analysis ToolPak'. Put a tick in the box and select 'ok.' To generate a random student selection, in a free cell, type '=randbetween(1, XX),' where XX equals the number of students in your class. Hitting 'enter' will produce a random number you can match to your Excel roster.

Besides establishing a solid questioning system, you should also focus on how you interact with the students when they do speak up. Listen to everything that she or he has to say. Be attentive, nod, and use some back-channeling (e.g., "uh-huh," "right," or "okay") to encourage your students' responses. Regardless of what the student says, try to connect the student's ideas with the answer you were seeking. If the student is completely off in left field, you might want to acknowledge the importance of her or his comment as it relates to another aspect of the class. Then, you might ask the student how their comment relates to the question at hand. Listening to their train of thought might teach you about your own questioning style and can be used to assess your teaching. Avoid telling your students "no" or "not really." If a student is behaving silly, this might be appropriate, but usually students are trying their best to produce an intelligent answer. By bridging their answer with the course material, you will redirect any unacceptable discussion or behavior in a positive manner. The key is to encourage your students and make them want to participate.

ASSESSMENT TECHNIQUES

Before getting to the graded assignments, let's talk about another way to cultivate a constructive classroom environment by developing a well-rounded system for assessing your students. Appropriate assessments can be motivating and allow students to track their progress. Your approach to assessments lets students know that their learning is the number one priority for your class and can heighten the seriousness with which students work with class material.

We like to think of assessments in two ways—informal and formal. There are assessments that take place after a lecture, reading, activity, or other teaching moment which you use to make sure students have a basic comprehension of the material at hand. These are known as "classroom assessment techniques" and their informal quality makes them fitting for use between formal assessments. The graded quizzes, exams, papers, presentations, and projects are the more traditional, formalized assessments that help you understand how well students understand the material.

Classroom assessment techniques have two goals: to help your students develop a sense of what and how they are learning; and to provide you with continuous feedback on student progress, what they liked about the material, and how your teaching style is helping or hindering their learning. Classroom assessment techniques come between the teaching (the lecture, reading, or group assignment) and the graded test, and offer a chance for both you as a teacher and your students as learners to better understand the relationship between teaching and learning.

There are many different types of classroom assessments. College teachers might apply a basic classroom assessment technique once or twice during the semester. At the high school level, frequent assessments will prove helpful, especially before a test review, so you have a better sense of how much time you need to dedicate to reteaching certain material. As for how to apply these techniques, it really depends on your students and class. You will quickly discover that even though you might be teaching two sections of the same course, at the same time, using the same materials and lesson plans, each class will react to and learn differently from you. The beauty of classroom assessment is that you can figure out why this is and what you can do to tailor your teaching to each class. Here are some examples of assessments compiled by biologist Douglas Eder (see info box):

INFO

For more great classroom assessment techniques, swing by:

www.siue.edu/~deder/assess/catmain.html

We also recommend: *Classroom Assessment Techniques: A Handbook for College Teachers* (1993) **by Thomas Angelo**

- **Directed Paraphrasing**
  In one to three clear, concise sentences, please write your definition of *XYZ*, or at least what you think it should be. Construct a definition that would make sense to your classmates.
- **The Muddiest Point**
  What has been the "muddiest" point so far in this session? That is, what about our discussion remains the least clear to you?
- **Group Effectiveness**
  Please answer all questions below from your own perspective. If you cannot answer a question, please state briefly why the information is unavailable.

  1. What specific goal(s) is this group trying to accomplish? Please list the goal(s) in *your* priority order. Do you think the group agrees on this list?
  2. What activities has the group undertaken in order to achieve its goals? Which activities, if any, are particularly effective?
  3. Does each group member have specific—even unique—responsibilities that help the group attain its goal(s)? List all group members by name and their individual responsibilities.
  4. Do you find the work of your group stimulating and worth your time? How many hours per week do you spend working with this group?

As you can see, the type of assessment really depends upon the context.

Regardless of the tool you choose, after you've collected and examined the student responses, you should *always* give feedback to your students, either individually or as a class. Make any adjustment you see necessary to your teaching, and let students know that the change came about as a result of their assessment. Teacher feedback, early and often, improves student answers, avoids teacher and student mistakes, and aids in classroom management by establishing you as a concerned, engaged teacher. Students know that they will have periodic opportunities to influence the flow of class. With regular feedback, students will come to enjoy helping you mold your teaching to fit their needs. They will also have a broader view of their role in the process of teaching and learning.

GRADED ASSESSMENTS

Earlier, we mentioned the importance of having different kinds of graded assignments. Generally, students prefer lots of little assignments rather than have their whole grade ride on one or two tests. Students also prefer a range of tasks. Poor test takers know they can count on doing well on a written paper to support their grade. As we noted in chapter 1, having a range of assessments also makes the classroom more accessible to students with learning disabilities or other special needs. Overall, a range of assessments provides a deeper, more meaningful student experience.

Let's see why having a variety of assessments might be important as a way to establish a grade that accurately reflects what your students have learned. Say the students' final grade is based on a midterm and final exam. Let's say you only give these two tests, and each test is worth fifty points (for a total of a hundred points). In this case, each point on each test is worth 1 percent of the students' grade. If a student is ill and performs poorly on one of the tests, the final grade might not accurately reflect the student's learning. By adding in other assessments, you maximize the possibility that your students' grades connect to the range of material you've covered and not some random event. Statistically, you will find that the more graded assessments you have, the more a student's overall average will stabilize (rather than fluctuate) after each assessment.

Diversifying your assessment tools can be easy. If you are a firm believer in the value of exams, you can still make them worth the biggest portion of the final grade, but also include a project, paper, or homework. Generally, tests shouldn't count for more than 75 percent of a student's grade, but don't be shy about making them count for less. Let's say you decide to make the tests worth 50 percent of the overall grade. Now, if you give your students a midterm and final, each will be worth only 25 percent. As for the other half of your students' grades, you can assign a paper worth 25 percent, and then have homework that covers the last 25 percent. Spreading the final grade out like this allows students who might get Bs on their exams to prove themselves on their paper and homework and still earn an A in the class. You can make as many categories as you feel necessary. You can also put in a category for attendance or participation as a way to help students who are putting in a lot of effort. Just be open about how you will grade effort-based assignments.

Now that we have you thinking about the overall grading scheme, here are some more ideas for individual assessments.

INFO

Want to minimize cheating on tests? Skim through these ideas:
http://illinois.online.uillinois.edu/resources/tutorials/assessment/cheating.asp

1. Tests
   - Traditionally, there are two types of questions on exams: objective and subjective. Both have their merit, and both have their downfalls. Objective questions (such as multiple choice, matching, or fill in the blank) are great for grading purposes but can be challenging to write. Sometimes, we think that the answers are obvious, but others might find them confusing. Students, forced to choose between ambiguous answers, will call the test "unfair." When writing objective questions, make sure that your question is clear and that your answers are not vague or misleading. If everyone in your class misses a certain question, consider removing that problem from the grade. Electronic grading programs can give you statistical information that will help you see whether a question had an inherent flaw.
   - With subjective questions (such as definitions, short answer, or essay), you will have to spend more time grading, but these give students an opportunity to talk their way through a problem and demonstrate exactly what they know. Subjective questions force students to engage material at a deeper level. Educators can better see what students have learned and whether the outcomes match the teacher's goals. Remember, a lucky guess can boost a grade on a multiple-choice test, leaving professors at a loss to know whether or not students actually learned the material.
   - When grading subjective assessments, make sure your students know what constitutes an A versus a B, or a C. Grading rubrics make subjective grading easier for you and more transparent for your students. Rubrics are a kind of checklist that includes the points you will examine to develop a final score. Ideally, the rubric shows students both whether they accomplished a task and how well they did so. You might think about developing the grading rubric alongside the test itself. This will force you to think about how you will grade before you have the completed test in hand. Early rubric development also allows you to give clearer directions to your students. You can distribute the rubric prior to the test, so students know well ahead of time what you expect from them. After the test, grading rubrics tell students exactly where they made a mistake, a point that gives them a way to improve their work in the future. Finally, in large classes, grading rubrics help you remember why you graded a paper or exam in the way you did in case students dispute their grade.
   - A few miscellaneous points about tests. Don't forget to ask yourself how long the students have to take the test. Will everyone be able to finish on time? If you want in-depth answers, you might want to give take-home tests. These can be longer and more demanding, but the students usually learn quite a bit during the process of com-

INFO

Check this site out for some cool ideas on developing rubrics:
www.teach-nology.com/web_tools/rubrics/

Customize your own rubrics at:
http://rubistar.4teachers.org

pleting the test. Work to create tests that discourage cheating. While subjective tests do this best, you can counter cheating on objective tests by handing out different versions of the test (you might order the questions in different sequences). After you have reviewed test answers with students, be sure to collect all test copies, so future students won't have access to your questions.

2. Homework
   - Homework can mean many different things. Any work that students complete outside class—beyond normal studying—can, and should, count. When thinking about what homework to assign, consider the difference between homework and busywork. Homework should be something that actively contributes to the students' learning. Busywork is time-consuming and redundant. Giving your students a list of vocabulary words and having them write out definitions is busy work. Having students find newspaper articles that exemplify vocabulary words is homework.
   - Other good examples of homework include having students go to a museum exhibit, asking them to see a particular movie and writing a thought piece about it, conducting interviews, collecting data for laboratory analysis, comparing different types of presentations on TV, and writing a book review.
   - Once you've decided on a few assignments, you should think about how many points you will give students for completing the assignment. If a task takes two or three hours to complete, you might want to make it worth more than something that students can finish in five minutes.
   - Think about how you will grade the assignments. Did the students do the work to the best of their abilities and still get some wrong answers? In such a case, the students probably deserve full credit. Or do the students' mistakes show that they threw the assignment together at the last minute? Regardless of how you decide to grade the assignments, homework is a powerful way for you to get your

students involved with your material outside of the classroom and be rewarded for it. In contrast to high-stress, high-stakes testing, homework allows students to learn material and improve their grade in a relatively relaxed setting.

3. Research Papers
   - Research papers are a great way to get students to focus on a specific topic and display what they've learned. The problem that you'll encounter is that many students have difficulty writing a research paper. The best thing you can do is give all of your students a thorough description of what you want. If you haven't been trained in teaching students how to write, think about contacting your campus writing center or colleague in the English department for help. A guest speaker trained in teaching students how to write could liven up the class and help you learn how to teach this material in the future.
   - Students are used to teachers having different writing requirements, so tell your students how you want them to structure the paper. You can give them an outline to follow while writing (e.g., I. introduction, II. literature review, III. methodology, IV. analysis, V. conclusion). Even though your categories might vary, give ideas of what to write in each section. Next, provide a sample bibliography and point out the differences between citing books, articles, magazines, websites, and other sources. This is also a good time to demonstrate how to cite within a text. Remember that generally, the most advanced college students can develop a thesis and defend it with appropriate evidence. Younger students will need help writing the paper regardless of the subject matter.
   - Few students voluntarily write drafts of their papers, even though this technique is one of the best ways to improve writing and critical thinking skills. You can fix this by working with your students through the multiple phases of paper writing. (This also helps avoid cheating.) Have students begin the process by handing in a proposal of what they want to write along with a few references. (You can also check their citation abilities here.) Next, have each student turn in an annotated bibliography and examples of any data that they are collecting. A few weeks later, students can either turn in a rough draft of their paper or an extended outline. At this point you can skim through the papers to make sure your students are on the right path, but don't correct anything. Instead, conduct a writing workshop in the class, where students read two or three of their peers' papers and make comments. This will lessen your workload and involve your students in the writing process.
   - When they turn in the final draft, you might want to have students include all of their work—the proposal, drafts, and data—in a kind

of portfolio. This collection lets you see the whole process of student development, provides a better learning experience for students, and makes it difficult for students to cheat. If you have a large class, papers written in multiple phases will produce an onerous amount of grading. In this case, you can have students write their papers in groups of two or three. In both large and small classes, the grading rubrics described above help both you and students understand what counts as a successful assignment.

4. Presentations
   * Regardless of your students' academic level, public speaking can be intimidating. If you want your students to do presentations, we recommend that you train them first. Have them do smaller, more informal presentations throughout the term. Show them some basic public-speaking techniques like standing up straight and projecting their voices. Give students the opportunity to practice with visual aids, and teach them how to use them. Another way to alleviate public-speaking anxieties is to have students participate in group presentations—just make sure that everyone contributes equally. (A peer evaluation can help you see how well students collaborated when you weren't looking.) You can ensure an attentive audience by including information from their presentations on your final exam! Again, use a grading rubric for presentations. Share your rubric with students ahead of time, so they can see just what qualities of the presentation you'll assess.

INFO

Here's a good example of a peer-based rubric for evaluating group presentations:

http://www4.nau.edu/assessment/oaalibrary/Rubrics/Group_Participation_Rubric.htm

5. Participation
   * If you include participation in your grading, we recommend that you make it as impartial as possible. While you will probably soon know exactly who participates and who doesn't, you'll want an objective way to translate your knowledge into a grade. One way is to include attendance as part of the students' participation grade. They might receive points for every attendance and lose points for each absence. Another technique is to tell students what counts as A-level participation versus B, C, or D, and then have students themselves

submit weekly or monthly reflections that assign themselves a grade (one you can adjust). The idea behind participation is to encourage your students to take an active and constructive approach to their education. Participation is a way to reward active learning and take into account much of the hidden work that takes place outside the classroom.

- While an objective system is the most straightforward, some teachers like to leave themselves a little more wiggle room when assessing participation. Basing a certain number of points (or percentage) of a student's grade on your personal assessment of their efforts allows you to reward students who you think deserve something extra. While this system works well in smaller classes, it is difficult to apply in large classes.

6. Extra Credit
   - Students enjoy extra-credit assignments and regularly request them. Our first inclination is to avoid them. If the students know that you offer extra credit, they may use it as a crutch to compensate for somehow missing out on your larger course goals. Nonetheless, carefully constructed extra-credit assignments can reward students eager to take their learning to the next level and allow you to put material in front of students that, otherwise, doesn't fit your schedule. If your grade includes very few assessments (e.g., the midterm-final approach), extra credit might be a good way for students to make up some ground. In either case, require the students put in real effort on the assignment and demonstrate what they've learned. Make sure that you don't offer too many extra-credit points. The extra-credit system isn't meant to be an incentive system.

RECORD KEEPING

By mid-semester you may be flooded with scores, attendance records, and other paperwork. A good record-keeping system will keep your class running smoothly. You'll be able to document any decisions you make about grading, attendance, and class participation. Also, students notice whether a teacher mislays papers, fails to recall assignments, or has trouble finding information. Organized teachers carry more authority in the classroom. A good record-keeping system will help in all your interactions with students.

The most important information to keep track of is students' grades. You have a few options here. Bookstores and school supply offices include an array of teacher grade books that also help you keep attendance. Keeping a written record of grades is a good idea, just in case your computer crashes. Many computer grading programs include features for weighting grades, tracking attendance, and keeping a database of students' personal information. If your school has an online grading system, you're in luck. Most of these programs are available for students to view as well, so they don't have to come to you to check on their grade. Even with such a great resource, it is still a good idea to keep a written record as a back-up.

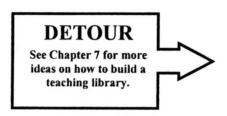

DETOUR

See Chapter 7 for more ideas on how to build a teaching library.

Seating charts are a time-honored way of keeping track of attendance. If your students will be remaining in assigned seats for a time, draw up a map of who sits where on a piece of paper. An empty seat can be easily compared with the chart to see who is absent. Keeping track of attendance gets trickier in a large class. The easiest way to record attendance here is to set up a spreadsheet with the students' names along the side and the dates of class across the top. Each class, pass the sheet around and have the students sign their initials for the appropriate date. Students could, otherwise, sign in on a single sheet of paper. If you're concerned about cheating on attendance, you could have in-class assignments that count as a record of attendance. You may also develop a policy that has a consequence for students caught cheating on attendance. Whatever method you use, spend a few minutes each week and record the attendance in your record book or on the grading program. Also, make sure that you file all of the signature sheets for future reference. While this might seem excessive, it will help you figure out grades, as well as give you a thorough record in case you need to drop or fail a student.

You will accumulate additional, miscellaneous paperwork including class rosters, add/drop sheets, grade sheets, doctors' notes, assignments students failed to pick up, and so on. Create a file for all this paperwork. Write the course name, year, and semester on the tab, and keep it for however long your program requires (in case someone later contests a grade).

Finally, make copies of all final grade forms before submitting them. If your school has an online grading system, make sure you print out a copy of the grades for your records. You never know who will dispute a grade, so keep everything.

STOP

Make sure you find out your
department's policy on
keeping your students' final
exams. Some departments
require you to keep them for a
set number of years.

FINDING HELP

Even though we have tried to provide as much practical information as possible here, you will probably run into some unanticipated problems with your students. Teaching—at any level—offers continuous surprises. If you run into a situation you are not sure how to handle, you have a few avenues for help. First, seek out people who seem skilled in working with students and can offer a fresh perspective. You might ask your colleagues or chairperson for advice. They have likely run into similar situations and will be able to offer ideas, if not put the situation into a broader context.

INFO

**Here are two good spots dedicated to helping
teachers:**

www.sitesforteachers.com
www.pacificnet.net/~mandel

At the college level, you can also contact your school's center for teaching and learning. These centers help instructors with all types of problems and concerns and, on many campuses, act as a meeting ground for a school's most enthusiastic teachers. If the campus support center can't help you, they will be able to direct you to someone who can. For high school teachers, try asking your mentor teacher, your department chairperson, administrator, or curriculum and instruction office for direction. The key to solving a problem is not to panic. There is always a way to find help.

TO DO LIST

1. Prepare some classroom management strategies.
2. Develop a plan for questioning techniques.
3. Figure out what assessments you are going to use (and why).
4. Find a grading program that works for you.

6

Tenure and Promotion for College Professors

Getting to Full 101

While most of this book has addressed the day-to-day aspects of teaching, new college professors will almost always keep in mind the long-term teaching prize: tenure. Attending to both your teaching and other academic duties in ways that assure you tenure can make for a tricky balancing act. In this book, we've tried to simplify and demystify the teaching. Now, it's time to bring in some other professorial duties and suggest ways to build bridges between your teaching and the rest of your academic life.

It helps if, at this point, you ask yourself what kind of professor you want to be. Some schools will answer that question for you. Depending on where you land a job, teaching may count for as little as 20 to 40 percent of your overall duties or as much 80 or 90 percent. Whatever your situation—and investigate carefully the campus scuttlebutt that tells you what *really* counts toward your tenure—if you've picked up this guide, you're probably not willing to sacrifice quality teaching for the research and service aspects of your job. The good news is that you don't have to. This chapter gives you tips on how to balance strategically your obligations inside and outside the classroom.

INTEGRATING RESEARCH AND TEACHING

If you're lucky enough to have landed that dream job, the one that allows you to teach courses that directly apply to your research interests, then integrating research and teaching becomes much simpler. You can assign reading materials to your students that also help you refresh your memory or stay current in the literature. You can organize group and independent student projects that delve into the topics closest to your interests. Students are sure to spot new developments, up-and-coming colleagues, and exciting publications. Classroom activities can even contribute toward your publication record. We heard of one professor who organized a graduate class around the publication of an edited book. Each student in the class contributed one chapter to the volume! Professors whose work requires field research often organize field schools precisely because this student support allows them to maintain an ongoing presence in their research site.

In any case, whenever your students are conducting independent research, be sure they showcase their findings. Steer them toward disciplinary conferences that are welcoming to undergraduates. (Some conferences offer sessions dedicated to undergraduate presentations.) Consider student-friendly publishing outlets. Coauthor with your students where appropriate. And, don't hesitate to promote student work to colleagues. While your students shine, you can bask in reflected glory.

But, what if you find yourself covering three or four sections of an introductory course every year? What if your teaching includes a general education requirement that simply falls outside your area of expertise? While you may not be able to spend as much time as you like on your favorite topics, you can, still, talk about your work in ways that enrich the class and excite students. Broad survey courses often include ancillary materials (e.g., movies, books, and articles), and you can select these to reflect your expertise. Use these materials to demonstrate the overarching themes in the class. Survey classes also offer the opportunity for you to use presentations that you have delivered (or will present) at conferences. Not only will this show the applicability of your research, you demonstrate to students your credibility in your field and that, like them, you are undertaking a journey of discovery. Students in any course will enjoy learning the hidden secrets of your research (the lab experiment that went awry! the unexpected answers on the survey instrument!), because it gives them a feeling of being close to the research enterprise.

REST STOP

At the very beginning of your career, consider repeating the same class as much as possible. This minimizes time spent on planning and grading. It also allows you to focus on technique rather than content and refine your skills in your chosen teaching style.

Perhaps the closest students can come to being part of the research enterprise is to conduct their own investigations or analyze aspects of your work. Even in introductory courses, you can posit for students a problem that is perplexing you, an obstacle you're trying to surmount. Bring in a guest speaker—one of your collaborators or someone with whom you'd like to develop a connection. You might even record the guest lecture for student analysis at a later date. Students in introductory, survey courses and students specializing in topics somewhat different from your own may not demonstrate expertise, but never underestimate the outsider's fresh perspective or insightful analysis. Put your material out there to the extent you can and see how students respond.

We have just talked about incorporating your research into your teaching. Now, we ask, might you want to make your teaching part of your actual research? We hinted at this above. Not a few professors turn teaching itself into a component of their research in ways that benefit both teachers and students. Some disciplines have a well-developed tradition along these lines. Math and science education come to mind. Your field may have a group of people whose interest in teaching your topic has become a research area in its own right. If your field is less developed in this regard, you might explore what other fields have to tell you about how to create a new area of expertise in your discipline, teaching!

INTEGRATING TEACHING AND SERVICE

Few graduate programs prepare people for the service requirements of the academic positions—making this one aspect of the job that can come as quite a surprise. Who knew so much time could be taken up by debating parking fees (if you're on a parking committee), or overseeing a college Web site (if you're on a public relations committee), or administering awards for undergraduate achievement (if you're on an awards committee)? This list could go on and on and on. It turns out, colleges and universities are run by committees. Technically, your participation on these committees is voluntary. Usually, you'll be *asked* to participate, and, unlike your teaching duties, nowhere in your job description does it say how many committees or service appointments are required of you. In practice, it can be very difficult to decline these requests. How do you say "no" to the chair of your department and future reviewer of your tenure file?

That's why oft-heard advice to new professors is to learn how to say no. Experienced professors understand that committee assignments can be a time sink. If service is 20 percent of your job description, that should equal one-fifth of your time or one day out of the week. Yet, committee assignments can quickly balloon to take up two and three days of your week. New professors are especially vulnerable to service assignments as senior professors may be anxious to get rid of their own, weighty commitments. Is there a workable option between saying "no" to service requests and ingratiating yourself to the point where your teaching and research suffer?

We offer two approaches to this question. The first is, again, to think precisely about your teaching and research interests. Then accept or seek out service assignments that complement or boost your work in these areas. If you're interested in learning new teaching techniques, then a service assignment that connects you to the campus's teaching support center may be welcome. If you're excited by the prospect of developing a new degree or certificate in your field, then you'll want to sit on the curriculum committee and learn how programs make it through the bureaucracy to final approval. If you're interested in connecting classroom learning to other campus activities, then a committee linked to the student dormitories or student clubs will offer you a way to justify the time you spend on this area.

The same idea follows for your research. If you're interested in environmental issues, then a seat on the committee that oversees the campus physical plant may allow you to "green" your campus. If you work on an unusual topic with few funding sources, you might work with the campus alumni organization to cultivate donors. All these ideas require a careful assessment of your own priorities, a careful understanding of your school's administrative structure, and a savvy awareness of how your preferred service commitments will be valued by the colleagues who will assess your tenure file. Are there areas of overlap between your interests and those of your senior colleagues? If so, build on these and be sure to advertise how you are advancing mutual interests.

The closer the integration across your research, teaching, and service, the less time-consuming any one aspect of your job is likely to be. Still, reading about this first approach, it should be clear that even when your service enhances the other parts of your job, the amount of time you commit to service can be considerable. So, in order to place a limit on the ever-expanding service possibilities, we suggest you keep a very detailed calendar. Most people use their calendars to schedule future appointments. We suggest you also use your calendar to document how you spend your time. List everything. During what time period did you grade papers? Write that article for publication? Go to that faculty meeting? Work on that committee assignment? Precisely, how much of your time is occupied by the different tasks that make up your working life?

The calendar helps you in a few ways. First, it lets you know where you might be more efficient with your time. Are you spending eight minutes grading a student's five-page paper? A grading rubric might cut that time in half and still give the student quality feedback. Does it take you a full day to prepare for one class session? You might work with your campus teaching center to structure a class that requires less preparation time and still delivers a quality education.

Perhaps most importantly, a detailed calendar will support you should you need to modify your service assignments or say no to additional service requests. Do you have so many assignments that you're in meetings three days a week? Do you feel so pressed for time that the idea of yet another assignment makes you want to disappear under your desk? A calendar lets you speak about these problems in objective terms with your supervisor and colleagues.

If your existing load is considerable, you might emphasize how much you want to help your program with these duties, but show why you're concerned with the amount of time occupied by your service. If your schedule is already full, you can respond to a new service request by, again, emphasizing how much you want to help. Follow this enthusiasm with a question

STOP

A tenure portfolio can include your C.V.; teaching, research, and service statements; course syllabi and student evaluations; copies of your scholarly work, and other materials. Save *everything* you can think of in your file.

about your full calendar. Is there a service assignment you could *replace* in order to accommodate this new request?

Remember, it's in your chair's interest to have committee assignments covered, but it's also in his or her interest that you create a successful tenure portfolio. Just as your students' success reflects well on you, your success reflects well on your department. By choosing a few assignments that closely relate to your interests and saying no to assignments that are simply beyond the time available in your schedule, you'll go a long ways toward proving yourself an amiable colleague and establishing an on-campus track record in your field.

GETTING HELP THROUGH COLLABORATIONS AND ASSISTANTS

The more you observe your successful colleagues, the more you'll see that few of them go it alone. Successful academics have built a support network that draws on different parts of the higher education community. During the first year on your job, you'll want to spend time getting to know both who will oversee your tenure application and who are the most *helpful* people who can provide support for your goals. Here, we offer three of the more usual directions in which faculty look for help. As you get to know your institution, other sources of help are likely to become evident. In this section, we leave out the campus teaching resources center. We figure these centers already top your list of teaching help. Instead, we focus on collaborations with your fellow colleagues, your work with teaching assistants (TAs), and, the people who really know the down and dirty, the office staff.

New faculty members often collaborate with colleagues on research and writing, so why not teaching? We've heard of colleagues assigned the same introductory class who jointly created lesson plans and effectively cut their preparation time in half. Because the two professors held different specialties, they divided the work to reflect each teacher's strength. Students had access to expertise they might otherwise have missed. Junior faculty members often form support groups to help them stay on track with their publications. Couldn't a teaching group help you spot potential problems in your syllabus, practice new teaching techniques, or simply decompress after a long week? In practice, lots of writing groups support both writing *and* teaching. While we imagine a teaching group as including non-tenured faculty members—to whom else can you admit your mistakes and your deepest teaching fears?—you might create a special place in your teaching/ tenure portfolio for collaborations with senior colleagues.

```
┌─────────────────────────────────┐
│  DETOUR                          │
│  Where should you store      ┐   │
│  all of your portfolio        \  ⟍
│  materials?  Learn more        \   ⟍
│  about building a teaching     /   ⟋
│  library in Chapter 7.        /  ⟋
│                              ┘   │
└─────────────────────────────────┘
```

Embarking on a joint effort with senior colleagues has a number of advantages for your teaching and your tenure application. As you know, when it comes to teaching, there's no substitute for experience, and senior colleagues have plenty of it. You can tap into this experience and simultaneously build an advocate for your tenure application. If there's a fellow faculty member known to work well with junior colleagues, you might coteach a course with this senior professor, who can then speak confidently and in detail about your own teaching abilities. If you'll be teaching a course that is also (or was formerly) offered by a colleague, meet to talk about which aspects of the course work best. Is there anything about the course he or she would change? Many professors will welcome the chance to share and be flattered that you value their work. And, by linking your own teaching to that of your colleagues, the future reviewers of your tenure package will feel an even greater interest in your success.

At the above mention of using teaching assistants to help your teaching, maybe you felt a spark of excitement or maybe you cringed. Were you one of the lucky teaching assistants who worked with the department's star professor? Were you one of those TAs who walked away from the TA assignment with a prepared course, an idealized model of what teaching can accomplish, and the motivation to take on your own class? Or, did your teaching assistantship entail dreary grading assignments, responsibility without authority, and an unappreciative undergraduate audience? Even if your own teaching assistant period was less than ideal, you probably learned an important lesson. Teaching assistants work best when they are *mentored* through the teaching process. By mentoring your TAs, you can draw on their enthusiasm and fresh approach to improve your classroom.

We think of teaching assistantships as a kind of internship, and we encourage you to approach your work with TAs as a time when you supervise future colleagues who are practicing a new craft. An internship is a structured, formal position that entails hands-on learning, an overall plan, assignments that build skills and knowledge, and, finally, some kind of assessment that explores the intern's ability to work independently in the field. Successful internships include ongoing supervision, so you'll want to delegate while maintaining supportive oversight. As with teaching, the more work you can put into designing the internship early on, the less of a workload you'll bear as the class progresses. And, as with teaching, you can repeat the experience. Invite successful teaching assistants to work with you in the future. If you're responsible for a class with multiple TAs, seek a mix of experienced and novice graduate students and encourage peer learning among your TAs.

We know one professor who created time for her research by developing a TA internship in which she oversees three graduate students each responsible for his or her own, semester-long class. The internship counted toward the professor's overall teaching load, but notice she only worked with the three TAs, not the ninety-plus students taking the TAs' classes. By working with the TAs as a group, the professor was able to enrich their experience by pointing out the different expertise they each brought to teaching. Because of the ongoing professional supervision and collective planning, students received a higher quality classroom experience. However you choose to work with TAs, we've learned the best measure of your own success are the graduate students themselves. You'll know you're doing a good job when graduate students approach you to request a position on your TA staff!

We mostly think of TAs as positions occupied by graduate students, but can undergraduates work as TAs? Most definitely. The goals of an undergraduate TA will be different, and so will the tasks you entrust to younger interns. Undergraduate TA internships are more likely to focus on leadership abilities (if they oversee discussion groups), interpersonal skills (if they handle miscellaneous student inquiries), organization and management (if they take attendance, maintain class files, or enter grades into a grade book), writing (if they act as a peer tutor on paper drafts), or the presentation of complex information in an accessible format (if they prepare a presentation or two). Senior-level undergraduates acting as TAs for introductory courses can also refresh their memory of the field's broad sweep while deepening their knowledge of a specific area (if they take responsibility for a class period or topic). In general, we discourage having undergraduates grade student assignments, as students are unlikely to trust that a peer has the knowledge for accurate assessment. As with graduate TAs, successful undergraduate teaching internships rely on planning and supervision. Also, as with graduate TAs, you'll want to be careful that you use your TAs' time wisely.

Supervising TAs requires some time on your part; however, you may find the benefits well worth it. You'll get help on tasks that are less motivating for you. In the company of people you like, a semester's coursework seems a lighter load. You create future colleagues whose own quality teaching may improve your classroom experience as they send you well-trained students. Collaborating with a TA can be both exciting and invaluable to your craft.

As you grow in your position as a faculty member, you may find that office staff count among your most valued and most underpaid colleagues. But, you may wonder, don't these folks just answer telephones, deal with the chair's needs, and pester faculty with bureaucratic demands? Not exactly. Depending upon how your particular department operates, office staff—including custodial staff—can help you with myriad teaching tasks, such as book orders, photocopies, and audiovisual equipment.

Beyond these tasks, office staff can help you understand how your department and your school operate. Office staffers retain an institutional memory that can help you make sense of both your own teaching and how your courses fit with broader departmental relations. Why are there three faculty qualified to teach a class, while the burden of the class tends to fall to the junior among them? Why are some classes having a hard time attracting students while other classes fill every seat in the room? What's the best tactic to take in order to have a course approved as a requirement for your major?

In working with office staff, it's important to keep a few things in mind. Structurally, the position of office staff is very different from that of faculty. While beholden to the department chair or an office supervisor, they are nonetheless besieged by requests for help from students and faculty alike. (This is, also, why they know so much—they see the whole departmental picture in ways you cannot.) A request preceded by the phrase "I'm not sure if this falls within your job description, but I'm wondering if . . . " will go a long ways toward shoring up goodwill among office staff. Amiable faculty who are sensitive to the demands office staff face will get more help from staff over the long run. Also, while privy to all kinds of information, staffers survive by employing high amounts of discretion. Office staff are unlikely to gossip, and, as a new faculty member, you should never put staff in the awkward position of saying something negative about your colleagues.

INFO

Learn proper professorial etiquette. Read Ms. Mentor's columns in the *Chronicle of Higher Education*. Read her book, *Ms. Mentor's Impeccable Advice for Women in Academia* (U. of Pennsylvania Press).

Instead, pose neutral questions that invite people who wish to share to do so. Revisiting the questions listed above, you might ask: "What's the history of the staffing of this particular class?" "I've noticed that some classes are more popular than others, what do you think best attracts students to any given class?" "I'm thinking it might be interesting to revisit the question of what we require for the major, but I'm wondering what conversations people may have had about this in the past." As you get to know the office staff, you will learn how their particular talents can help you in your teaching. We worked with one staffer who was so adept with a turn of phrase that she was our first resource in planning an awkward conversation with a student. Always communicate your thankfulness to office staff. Remember them during the holidays or on their birthdays, especially during your first year on the job, when you'll rely on these folks the most. Cherish good staff.

PUBLICIZING YOUR TEACHING

In higher education, it isn't always enough to be a good teacher. Professors often have to demonstrate their teaching qualities and explain their teaching philosophies in ways that make sense to outsiders. This makes it incumbent upon you to depict what goes on in your classrooms, your successes and failures, as well as your ongoing learning. Here we want to address three places where this depiction takes place, the statement of teaching philosophy, the annual reports you offer to your program that justify how you have spent your time, and the curriculum vitae (c.v.). The c.v. and the annual reports form part of your official record as a faculty member, and some schools include the statement of teaching philosophy alongside the other two. By working across the three formats, you'll build a language for explaining your work that you can use in other settings, in your service appointments, and in informal conversation with colleagues. These documents and these conversations make your teaching both visible and valuable to others. They form the cornerstones of your reputation as a teacher.

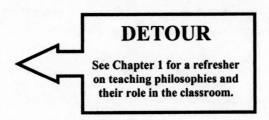

DETOUR

See Chapter 1 for a refresher on teaching philosophies and their role in the classroom.

Keeping an updated statement of your teaching philosophy, at least in the early years of your teaching, is helpful because the statement allows you to verbalize, in a central place and in a summary way, all the different aspects of your teaching. As a format, the statement of teaching philosophy is a little like the personal statements you wrote to get into graduate school.

While there are no set rules for how the statement should look, a glance at the postings on teaching websites across the country show a few trends. Generally, a teaching philosophy statement:

- is one or two pages long;
- uses the present tense and first-person voice;
- includes both your teaching ideas and practices in ways that allow the reader to imagine you in the classroom;
- is reflective of your own unique approach.

Beyond that, statement contents vary widely. We encourage you to read sample statements posted on the Web by professors from a number of different fields. The samples will give you a sense of the range of expression people display in their teaching statements, the ways writers balance general teaching concerns with disciplinary matters, as well as the phrasings people use to make their teaching come alive in print. Once you read the samples, you will likely find your own perspective clarified as you see the freedom the format offers to voice your individuality.

INFO

Check out Ohio State University for a description on how to develop a philosophy of teaching statement:

http://ftad.osu.edu/portfolio/philosophy/Philosophy.html

Your teaching statement forms a backdrop for the next writing task, your annual evaluations. Most institutions require professors submit a yearly accounting of their work. What classes did you teach, and how did students evaluate the classes? What research activities did you undertake, and what were the products of that work? What service assignments did you fulfill? Some annual evaluations are simple listings, but many include a narrative. In the narrative, you can explain to your colleagues the framework or antecedents of your year's work and where you'll be taking the work next. In other words, in the narrative portion of your annual reviews, you can employ brief references to your teaching philosophy to explain where you've been with your teaching activities and what future paths you expect.

Here's an example. Perhaps you started out your career with a teacher-centered philosophy, but wanted to try more learner-centered techniques. So, you took some workshops with your campus teaching support center, consulted with staff there to tweak an existing syllabus, and tried out a few learner-centered activities in a class that otherwise has been lecture-based. In your annual review, you might write up something along the lines of:

> In order to add to my skills as a lecturer, I spent five hours last summer in teaching workshops and in consultations with staff at the Campus Teaching Center. This allowed me to re-formulate two sections of my introductory course to include learner-centered activities. In these activities, students carried out and reported on brief field observations. The sections were successful, and students showed a greater enthusiasm for the course than in past semesters. In future iterations of the class, I plan to expand the learner-centered aspects of my teaching and continue to update my syllabus to reflect this new approach.

Notice how this statement conveys to readers that that the teacher has a clear sense of where she's coming from and where she's going. The statement demonstrates a willingness to learn and improve. All the while, that willingness has a direction, a philosophy. The reader can feel confident that these innovations are contributing to a bigger project.

While the curriculum vitae does not allow this kind of nuanced explanation, you can still use your vita to promote your teaching experience. The way to go about doing this is to treat the teaching section of your c.v. as you would a resume, with a few notations.

As you write this section of your c.v., think about the most pertinent information that a stranger to your career would want to know. Were you a TA or an instructor with sole authority over the class? How large was the class? In general, were students freshmen and sophomores (just beginning to learn your topic) or juniors and seniors (with more experience in the field)? What teaching method dominated the course delivery? What were the specific tasks you undertook, especially if you were responsible for only part of the class? In box 6.1, we offer two examples of this kind of narrative for your c.v. One example imagines a person who worked as a TA for a large lecture class. We use a bullet-pointed listing for this notation. The other shows the work of a teacher with independent authority over the class. We use a narrative style for this notation.

As time goes on, and as your teaching experience expands to the point at which a narrative proves too cumbersome for the c.v., you can still provide a general view of your teaching in a concise, readable manner. One format we find accessible to readers is the teaching chart. Table 6.1 is an example that quickly conveys the professor's suite of courses alongside the instructional formats with which the professors feels most adept.

Of course much more could be said about teaching and the c.v. If you're like many new faculty members, you obsess over the minutiae of the c.v., the font size, line spacing, and margins. You can make your life simpler and improve your c.v. by checking out the *Chronicle of Higher Education*.

BOX 6.1: PROFILING TEACHING IN THE C.V.

**Teaching Assistant, Large State University,
Introduction to My Field (Fall 2006-Spring 2007)**

- Conducted three discussion sections each semester of thirty students each
- Independently developed discussion materials and activities for X, Y, Z topical areas
- Collaborated with fellow TAs on the development of lecture, discussion materials, and activities for two additional topical areas
- Evaluated approximately 180 exams during each semester
- Advised students on note taking and study strategies
- Participated in ten hours of additional teacher training through campus support center with an emphasis on leading discussions and student advising.

**Instructor, Regional State University,
Senior Seminar in My Specialty (Fall 2009)**

I developed this course on My Specialty for an enrollment of approximately twenty-five students. In addition to choosing the topical information, I created student-centered lesson plans that emphasized formal and informal writing assignments, alongside discussion of these in small group format. I structured the course's culminating experience in the form of a group research project and organized a formal conference at which students presented their findings to the department.

The weekly publication occasionally includes a C.V. doctor's review under its "Career Talk" column. The doctor dissects and advises on the vita of academics in different fields and at different stages in their careers. We find the C.V. Doctor demystifies the format, and its useful suggestions give a strong sense of how others will read your vita.

Table 6.1. Courses Taught, 2005 to Present

Semester	Course Title	Level/Enrollment	Format
Fall '05, Spring '06	Introduction to My Field	Undergraduate/80-150	Lecture
Fall '06, '07	Theory for Majors	Undergraduate/30	Seminar
Spring '07, Spring '08	Senior Capstone	Undergraduate/15	Independent Research
Spring '08	Graduate Seminar on My Specialty	Graduate/5	Seminar/ Practicum

> ## INFO
>
> **Skim through Chronicle of Higher Education
> and its C.V. resources at:**
> http://chronicle.com/jobs/tools/

OKAY, BUT ISN'T TEACHING DEATH TO TENURE?

We've spent this chapter talking about integrating the different parts of your academic career, finding help with your teaching and publicizing your teaching through your statement of teaching philosophy, your annual evaluations, and your c.v. But, maybe you have a lingering doubt. Maybe you are, or want to be, in a setting that premises research over teaching. Maybe senior colleagues have reminded you of the adage (that makes us cringe) that a teaching award doesn't get you tenure. Surveying all the different kinds of higher education settings, we're happy to note that, if this is, indeed, your situation, you are in a minority. The vast majority of higher education settings in the United States want to see their students succeed, and administrators and faculty, alike, understand that quality teaching is the key to student success. If this just doesn't seem to be your situation, short of changing schools and finding a better fit for you, is there something you can do?

If you are truly stuck between the teaching rock and the research hard place, we suggest you do something contradictory to the advice usually given to young academics. New faculty are regularly advised to advertise their successes and increase their visibility in the field. If you have good reason to think successful teaching will hurt your career, we suggest you continue to excel as a teacher, only quietly and without fanfare. If your colleagues only seem to care for where, what, and how often you publish, then pointedly share this news with them. If your career is being measured by the size of your grants, you need not advertise the innovative outreach and education component that clinches your awards. Certainly, you should report those fantastic teaching evaluations when appropriate. However, for the most part, your teaching can act as source of personal satisfaction rather than public acclaim.

DETOUR

**Chapter 7 provides more
details on how to handle
evaluations.**

That is, until you get tenure. At that point, you'll be freer to be the kind of academic you want to be. As one of our advisors asked, "Now that you have tenure, what are you going to do with it?" Tenure is a time when you can re-direct your career, take a risk, push your interests to a new level. Tenure is the gold ring of the academic merry-go-round. Once you have it hand, you may choose to educate a generation of students who go on to become thoughtful, inquisitive colleagues, neighbors, citizens, and fellow travelers in life.

TO DO LIST

1. Develop a calendar to keep track of your hours.
2. Form a teaching support group with fellow faculty.
3. Create a teaching internship for graduate and undergraduate students.
4. Add teaching information to your c.v.

7

Tenure and Promotion for High School Teachers

Advancing Your Career 101

With some teachers estimating that each hour of class time requires two hours of preparation, it's no wonder that new high school teachers can be caught up in the day-to-day challenge of on-the-job learning. Additionally, in the classroom, new teachers might be surprised to find their pupils are less than appreciative of all this work. Recent findings on the teenage mind show that, yes, high school students do think differently from adults. Especially in their first year, untrained teachers can find themselves caught between instructional demands and the interpersonal dynamics created by students' changing personalities. Here, we talk about where to find the help that will make the first year a little smoother and set you on the path to a satisfying teaching career.

We address some of the issues found to contribute to teacher turnover—student discipline, support from school colleagues, and salary concerns (Ingersoll 2001). Because we want to offer a long-term perspective, we also consider tenure, the benefits of continuing education, as well as the creation of your own teaching library. Whether your teaching road starts off smooth or rocky, we encourage you to focus on consistent, incremental improvements. For teachers, as well as students, the classroom is a place of learning and adjusting. Track your improvements on a calendar to remind yourself how far down the teaching path you have traveled to date. Celebrate the accomplishments for which you have worked so hard!

"DO YOUR TEENS SEEM LIKE ALIENS?"

The PBS documentary series *Frontline* posed this question, clearly expecting an affirmative answer. The National Institute of Mental Health calls the teenage brain a "work-in-progress," one undergoing significant neurological change. This is a complex and growing area of research whose implications for the classroom are worth a brief exploration. Many student discipline problems are rooted in healthy and naturally occurring changes in a teenager's body. These changes can be complicated by stressors in a student's home or community life. As a teacher, you cannot be responsible for events taking place beyond the classroom, but you can adopt a few strategies that communicate to students a model for positive, adult behavior. As we explain, you can be fair, firm, and professional in your dealings with students.

> ### INFO
>
> **For more resources on the teenage brain and**
> **see our website:**
> Chapter 7

This approach counteracts the seesaw of personality characteristics that some teenagers experience. On the one hand, teenagers tend to need more sleep than adults (first-period teachers, beware!). On the other, teenagers can experience bursts of energy that leave them restless. (A student-centered classroom can help students express and channel this energy toward learning.) In the high school years, adolescents can veer between abstract, future-oriented thought and an inability to see beyond the present moment. As cliché as it may sound, experimentation, risk-taking, and a rebellious demand for independence are all part of normal, adolescent development (see info box).

Given the amount of time teenagers spend in school, teachers will see their students undergo dramatic changes. Waiting these out often proves valuable. By their senior year in high school, many teens will begin to look a lot like the adults we hope they will become. Along the way, some students might find a love of your subject matter—literature, history, science—to be just the passion that helps them weather teenage storms.

In the meantime, your fair, firm, and professional demeanor as a teacher will provide a measure of order to a setting marked by teenage changeability. All classrooms require a set of basic rules that foster learning. In creating your classroom rules (as well as consequences for rule-breaking), focus on issues of fairness for both the group and individual students.

REST STOP

Here are a few sample classroom rules:

1. No late work.
2. One person speaks at a time.
3 No more than 2 people out of their seats at a time.

The best rules are specific (so students know where they stand) without being overly rigid (you'll want to spend your time teaching rather than enforcing onerous rules). They address those elements you require to keep a well-run classroom, while striking a balance with teenagers' need for independence. Systematize your rules, so you're not in the position of inventing new ones for each situation students present. You'll earn students' respect when they see that you have organized your classroom in anticipation of their needs and are occasionally willing to take into account exceptional personal circumstances.

CAUTION
In September, you might change a few rules to be fair, but by March students will be questioning *all* your rules.

Importantly, once you've established your rules, make sure these are posted in an accessible place (the Web makes this information available at all times) and be calmly committed to carrying them out. Fair rules require *firm and consistent* implementation. Adolescents are masters of testing limits and pushing an adult's buttons, again part of the natural maturation process. If your rules contain a loophole or merit an exception, you can be sure that one of your students will bring this fact to your attention. Keeping in mind questions of fairness, you need not be swayed by students' persuasive arguments. You can acknowledge a student's objection to your rules, "This argument makes a good case for change," and still stand by your decision, "Nonetheless, this semester, the papers will be five pages in length." Your commitment to your fairly constructed rules fosters a predictable atmosphere where students can grow and learn. Students know in advance the effects of breaking the rules, and they can judge for themselves whether or not they want to incur those consequences.

The key to success in being fair and firm is the demeanor you bring to interactions with students. Adolescents are keen observers of human nature. They will note and react to any expression of negative emotions, such as anger, condescension, exasperation, or self-doubt. If any of these tempt you, give a boost to your professionalism by taking the communications advice offered by child psychologists Robert and Jean Bayard (1986). Employ a flat tone of voice, and speak to students in brief statements that avoid the word "you." (This lessens the possibility that the student will take your reaction as a personal accusation.) In uncomfortable situations with students, engage in the kind of speech and conduct that would be appropriate in your dealings with colleagues. By speaking with students in a respectful and professional way, you model the kind of behavior you seek from them.

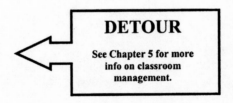

DETOUR

See Chapter 5 for more info on classroom management.

In their first year on the job, new teachers will likely be practicing their own personal style of fair, firm, and professional. It can take some time to understand just what will work given your own personality and the particular makeup of a school's student body. Rest assured that, even if you hit a few potholes, the benefits to this approach accrue over time, as you gain a reputation among students. Students will respect you more and test your limits less once they know you are fair, yet not easily swayed to change the rules. Overall, your fair, firm, and professional approach to students will downplay any teenage turmoil at hand and allow everyone to concentrate more on scholastics.

GETTING HELP FROM MENTORS,
ADMINISTRATORS, PARENTS, AND OTHERS

Whether or not you are assigned an official mentor and join a school-sponsored mentoring program, use your first months at a school to figure out who can best help you navigate the demands of your new job. Here, we describe the help you can expect from supportive mentors, administrators, school districts, and state offices. Parents can also be some of your strongest allies in steering a student toward higher learning. In working with your new advisors, stick to the question of "How can I do a better job?" Your first year on the job, it's easy to get caught up in workplace politics and family dramas, but you have enough to handle in the classroom. Focus on the kind of support that improves your work with all your students.

Your mentor will be the first person you turn to in order to learn how your school works in practice. Mentors can give advice on everything, from the mundane—what clothing is considered appropriate for teachers in your school—to the practical—such as time-management tricks—to the unwritten rules of school life—which extracurricular events are effectively required of faculty. A good mentor combines knowledge of official policies and procedures with unofficial school norms. He or she is willing to work with you on a weekly basis to address questions and problems as they arise. If your school doesn't assign you a mentor, seek one out. If you need more help than your mentor can offer, informally explore other teachers for their knowledge and willingness to share. Join or create a peer group of new teachers who can share their collective learning.

One way to cultivate supporters is to observe them in class. Peer observations are required by some schools. To build your support network, ask your students who their favorite teachers are. Most teachers would be flattered if you asked them to observe their classes (but definitely avoid drop-in visits). Even though your prep hour is a great time to take care of grading, planning, and catching up on email, it is also a good time to observe others. Consider dedicating one day a week to making observations. Take detailed notes about what worked in the classes and jot down ideas to incorporate into your lessons. Follow up your observation with an informal conversation. Here, you'll want to expand the conversation to see whether your new colleagues are good guides to your school and the overall teaching process.

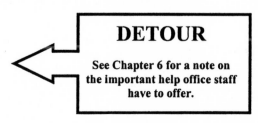

DETOUR

See Chapter 6 for a note on the important help office staff have to offer.

Administrators offer a different kind of support for your work. Turn to administrators whenever a problem arises that may require their attention, such as a discipline issue or a dilemma with a parent (more on that in a moment). Administrators always appreciate advance warnings. Administrators also help with scheduling issues. Maybe you have forty-two students in one section and just fifteen in another. As we describe below, administrators are the people who handle the formal evaluations that are so important to your long-term success. Cultivate administrators by asking them about teaching methods and lessons they've learned from years of experience. This work will bear fruit at that crucial moment when administrators discuss hiring and re-hiring decisions. In some cases, issues of confidentiality prevent administrators from speaking to you about your specific case, but always keep them in the know about your hopes and plans. If yours is a short-term position, let your administrators know you want to return. Drop by their offices a few times, so they can see your enthusiasm.

In your immediate teaching life, your school district and state offices might not figure prominently. However, these offices can include support services beyond the means of any school's limited budget. As you plan for continuing education, turn to the state and district for questions you have about certification and continuing education credits. Also, look to any regional education centers that your state sponsors for an expansive lending library that includes curriculum and instruction materials. If you think one of your students has special needs—such as speech or hearing therapy—the regional education center may be able to provide this service.

At the high school level, teachers can have an ambivalent relationship toward parents. After all, they only tend to see parents when a child is doing very well (usually supported by very involved parents) or when a child is doing poorly (when disciplinary issues or failing grades require parents' intervention). In either case, parents can be a powerful ally in your work to improve a student's education. Even if you must contact a parent for distasteful reasons, approach the conversation as an opportunity to learn what might be going on behind the scenes in your student's life. Work to make these encounters as positive as possible.

For example, if a student's grade suddenly turns sour or if a student seems distracted and uninterested in class, telephone the parent and calmly say as such. Notice how the parent responds. A parent under stress is likely to give you an earful. Their expression of frustration can be a necessary step to a more thoughtful conversation, so take their remarks in stride. If a parent disagrees with your assessment, have data on hand that corroborates your points, "Three times this week, I've asked him to put away his cell phone because he was spending time text messaging rather than paying attention to class." Experienced teachers often keep a "Family Contact Log" that details a student's behavior by date and reports the results of any attempt to speak with parents. You may not be able to resolve the problem. But, you can open a path of communication with a student's parents, learn about events that help you make better sense of a student's performance, and alert parents to additional resources at their disposal. It's always safe to advise a visit to your school's guidance counselor.

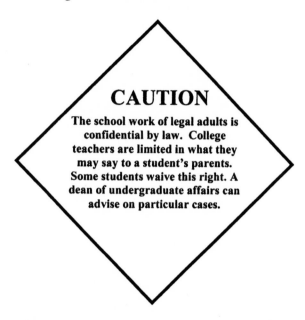

CAUTION

The school work of legal adults is confidential by law. College teachers are limited in what they may say to a student's parents. Some students waive this right. A dean of undergraduate affairs can advise on particular cases.

Regardless of how the student responds, parents can support your efforts, so don't put off talking with them. If a situation needs attention, and your own first attempts at resolution have failed, contact the parents. In the least, you'll gain some perspective on the situation. At the most, your work with a student's parents can send the message that the adults in his or her life are unified in their educational concerns.

BEING EVALUATED:
TENURE AND CLASSROOM OBSERVATIONS

Just like at the college and university levels, achieving tenure at the high school level ensures job security. Unlike college and university contexts, earning tenure at the high school level does not entail a weighty amount of publishing and professional service. Instead, at the high school level, tenure applications revolve around your classroom performance, your reputation (which you cultivated while getting help from mentors, administrators and your school district), and, to a lesser extent, your contribution to the broader community through extracurricular activities.

In this section, we outline how you should approach in-class observations. Additionally, high school teachers working under a bargaining agreement should look to this document to describe their pre-tenure time and requirements for achieving tenure. Remember, during your pre-tenure service, and based upon that agreement, your school's administration may not be obligated to renew your contract. Furthermore, you may be let go without a specific reason—an end which only happens to really poor or unprofessional teachers. After achieving tenure, the administration cannot relieve you of your position without following procedures which generally entail putting you on an improvement plan and closely monitoring you over a long period of time. The only conditions that qualify for permanent termination include some type of illegal—or professionally outlandish— activity or violation of the community's social mores.

STOP

No matter how tedious and
dull, your contract or
bargaining agreement is
required reading.

Let's consider those classroom observations. You'll want to be carefully prepared for these events. Having an administrator sitting in the back of your room with a clipboard, furiously jotting down notes, can quickly throw you off of your game—if you let it. Most administrators will let you know when they are planning an observation, although there is a growing trend toward unannounced, drop-in observations. Once you find out when you're going to be observed, there are a few points to take into account.

- Lesson Plans: Regardless of how abbreviated you generally make your lesson plans, you should be very detailed and formal (type them on the computer) on the day of your observation. Even if the observer doesn't ask to see your plans, make sure he or she receives a copy *before* class begins. You should also email the observer a copy of your lesson plan the day before any scheduled visit. In your lesson plan, for every activity or topic you cover, list the specific state and/or district standard that your teaching meets.

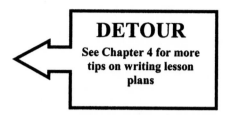

DETOUR

**See Chapter 4 for more
tips on writing lesson
plans**

- Content: When being observed, include a mix of new and old material. A quick review of previous lessons will showcase your students' progress and demonstrate their active learning. (Avoid designing your entire lesson around review material. This might bore the students and result in unnecessary management issues.) The new material in your lesson will hold the students' attention and highlight your teaching skills. Take care here not to introduce something too difficult. You will have other opportunities to experiment with complex material while administrators are sitting comfortably in their offices. And, as a back up, keep an extra, short piece of material or activity on hand. As we describe below, students will be on their best behavior during the observation, which usually means you will cover material faster than you planned.
- Routine: The biggest mistake new teachers make when being observed is trying to accomplish too much. The best way to ensure a good flow to your lesson is to maintain a classroom environment that is familiar to you and your students. Integrate your most popular—and frequently used—activities. Put your students in situations in which they are comfortable. Don't change the seating arrangement, nor should you try out new media. Not only can technological difficulties slow up your class, the administrator might think you're wasting time.
- Students: Unless you have poor rapport with your students, they will likely be on their best behavior during an observation. There are different ways to prepare students for an observation. Some teachers like to tell their students when they are going to be observed. We've even heard of teachers practicing a lesson with their classes before the administrator arrives. Rehearsing can backfire by elevating student anxieties. Instead, you might simply mention that an administrator is going to attend class because she or he is interested in how the students are doing. Another strategy is to avoid telling students about the observation at all but do explain the observer's presence when he or she arrives. Some teachers invite the administrator to observe their best

or favorite class—especially for the first observation. Should students misbehave during the observation, don't get frustrated. React with your usual management strategies. If students are reluctant to ask questions, become confused, or aren't overly enthusiastic that day, have no fear. Administrators like to see how you react to such normal situations. The key is consistency. Treat those circumstances as you do every day, and the administrator will be satisfied.

- Evaluation: After your observation—sometimes directly after—your administrator will sit down with you and review the official evaluation sheet. No matter what your observer says or how critical she or he is, do not be defensive. Even though you might not agree with the evaluation sheet, making excuses will only annoy the administrator. Instead, take the opportunity to ask for advice and get different perspectives on your teaching. You might even try this if you receive an excellent evaluation. Administrators have been around the block a few times, and they like to see someone who is interested in learning new techniques. Finally, if you have a difficult class (e.g., academically, personally, or with management), you might want to invite the administrator to conduct the evaluation during that specific class. Tell the administrator that you are having difficulties, and that you'd appreciate some feedback. In most cases, sympathetic administrators will focus in on your strengths during a challenging class and admire the fact that you went to them for advice.
- Drop-in Evaluations: While official evaluations can be rather nerve-racking, you should also be prepared for unofficial visits. Administrators like to see how you manage your class on any given day. (This is another reason why you shouldn't teach out of the ordinary for your official evaluation. The contrast will be noticeable.) If you have an unexpected visit by an administrator, remain calm and greet her or him upon entering your classroom. You might even take the opportunity to ask your class if anyone can tell your guest what you are studying. You can ask the administrator if she or he has any insight into the topic. Most administrators were once classroom teachers and relish the chance to demonstrate their teaching abilities. If you can get the observer to participate, you will have successfully engaged your visitor and taken the pressure off yourself. If you are in the middle of a busy class or small-group activity, you might want to walk over to the administrator and explain what you are doing. Don't be shy about inviting the administrator to help with your class. In the rare case that a district superintendent or assistant superintendent visits your class, they will remember your enthusiasm and constructive environment if you can get them to participate.

Even if you have a disappointing experience during an evaluation, rest assured you will have other opportunities to prove your teaching merit. New teachers are evaluated at least once a semester. Over three years, you can expect a minimum of six evaluations! Check with your district requirements to see how many observations you can expect. The purpose of official evaluations is to chart your progress and make sure that you are doing an adequate job. Administrators just want to see improvement or the potential for improvement, and you can concentrate your efforts on the same.

If you remain unsatisfied with your evaluations, there are other ways to demonstrate your abilities to the administration. Invite them to visit your classroom for student presentations, class projects, or during a particularly interesting lesson. You can also give them copies of your students' work (e.g., reports, projects, or even tests). The more they visit your class, the more comfortable you and your students will become. As long as your administrators and fellow teachers know that you are doing a good job on an average, daily basis, a few subpar evaluations won't stand in the way of your earning tenure.

EXTRACURRICULAR PARTICIPATION

As a high school teacher, you will have no shortage of opportunities to be involved beyond the classroom. For tenure purposes, some extracurricular events are necessary, as they allow you to get to know your students on a more personal level and make your work known to teachers, administrators, and community members who don't get to see you on a daily basis. Earning tenure and creating a positive reputation for yourself is much easier when the broader school community sees you are interested in more than just teaching. Also, extracurricular activities often bring a salary addendum. As with college service requirements, the key here is to choose activities that fit your personal interests. If your own interests aren't represented in the school's list of sport teams and clubs, look into starting a new group. If that sounds like too much work, think creatively about how you can adapt your interests to existing clubs.

For example, if you are a sports fan, ask about coaching opportunities. Even if no official coaching positions are available, rare is the head coach who wouldn't gladly accept a volunteer coach, athletic trainer, or statistician. Being involved in athletics is also a good way to meet and develop relationships with parents. Athletics tend to be the area where high schools are most likely to interact with the local community.

A well-rounded high school needs an array of extracurricular activities that provide students a chance to take on leadership roles, explore topics that may go uncovered in the curriculum, or take their interests to a deeper level. Your talent in music could provide a boost to an after-school arts program. If you're interested in working with community members and parents, ask about the district's PTA (parent-teacher association) or maybe even the booster club. We've heard of teachers who encouraged a knitting club, a model United Nations, and a Gay-Straight Alliance student group. Just be aware of becoming overcommitted—you don't want them to take away from doing a good job in the classroom!

Your colleagues are likely involved in a number of political or administrative groups that offer a different outlet for your talents, either within your school or at the district level. If curriculum issues fascinate you, tell an administrator that you'd like to be involved with the curriculum design team. Some districts even have oversight committees that discuss and vote on different school policies. You may want to join a professional book discussion after school or start a group of your own. If your goal is to get to know the other teachers in your school, you can easily find out who is on the faculty entertainment committee, who organizes faculty parties and happy hour events.

Outside your school district, being involved with groups working on a state or national level will expose you to other concerned professionals and help you network on a larger scale. Ask around and find out who is the local representative for the state teachers' union. Become a member of a professional association within your teaching content area. Frequently, such associations are involved in processes that influence standards and curriculum issues on the state and national levels.

The more you invest in your school and students, the faster you will establish yourself as an invaluable part of your district's community. Although it might take you a little longer to hone your teaching skills, by being proactive about participating in other aspects of your career, you will send a strong message about your professional aspirations. Extracurricular work, conducted in the spirit of openness toward new ideas, will reflect your sincere interest in education.

CONTINUING EDUCATION AND SALARY

While earning tenure is important, there are other aspects of the high school teacher's career that have a bigger impact on overall success—financially and professionally. Teacher salaries are closely tied to both years of experience in the field and efforts at continuing education. Financially, teaching rewards longevity and a continued interest in improving your teaching skills. Here, we offer a few tips aimed at improving your salary and providing you some flexibility over the course of your career, while you also keep your classroom fresh and innovative.

Most districts adhere to a fairly standard method of configuring pay scales which takes into account the number of years you've been teaching combined with the number of post-graduate credits you have accumulated. For example, new teachers with a bachelor's degree enter this scale at the lowest rung. The following year you might receive a bump in salary that reflects your experience. Some districts have started giving experience raises every three or four years.

REST STOP

To receive credit for your continuing education, make sure all the paperwork has been submitted properly. Keep copies of any evidence required by your administrators. Occasionally check with the appropriate office to make sure previously approved credits remain valid. Clerical mistakes happen, but you'll have the documentation to fix them.

While you can't make time move any faster, you can improve your financial position and your classroom teaching by taking courses for college credit or by earning post-graduate degrees. Because many districts reserve the right to approve or disapprove courses, check with the human resources office regarding acceptable opportunities. Here are a few points to keep in mind when you have this conversation.

Local universities, colleges, and regional education centers often sponsor district or school workshops, conferences, or classes that can count toward college credit. Teachers are frequently required to attend these to comply with state rules that seek highly qualified instructors. Sometimes, it is possible to pay a fee and do a little extra work to receive college credit for these obligatory professional growth requirements! Earning one or two credits for a workshop might not seem like much, but they do add up over the years.

Teachers' schedules can make it challenging to take traditional college courses toward a master's degree. However, many universities are rapidly expanding their online courses to meet the needs of working professionals. As you explore these and other opportunities, keep in mind that district and state requirements may not be the same. For example, it is possible for a course to count toward state requirements and, yet, not toward your district's increase in pay. Choose carefully to get the most out of your efforts.

In making your continuing education selections, think about advancing your career as well as your salary. A wise teacher is prepared to change positions within the school system, and the key to moving is holding multiple certifications. English teachers can become certified as math teachers, and classroom teachers can become certified to occupy supervisory positions. As you plan for your continuing education, seek courses that overlap as much as possible with a new and valuable certification.

BUILDING A TEACHING LIBRARY

Over time, you'll be juggling two sources of teaching information. One is your own experience with the classes you teach. The second is the myriad teaching tips you'll encounter in books, from colleagues, at conferences, and from your own growing body of experience. Bringing these two sources of learning together in a teaching library or a filing system will help create a teaching routine while providing a personalized source for ongoing help and inspiration. Our own teaching libraries include a few of our favorite books on teaching, a binder for each class we've taught, and a binder divided into teaching topics such as "interactive lectures," "asking questions" (to spark classroom discussions), "assessment techniques," "diversity and universal design," and "conducting seminars." This general-purpose binder includes handouts from teaching workshops, handwritten notes, and webpage printouts. Your own archive can be tailor-made for your teaching duties and styles, perhaps with sections on "labs," "field research," "writing exercises," and "grading rubrics." While we like to see things on paper, you might work well with electronic files. Over the long run, a teaching library allows you to formalize your knowledge and see your improvements over time. In the short run, the binders focusing on individual classes are likely to be the most helpful for you.

You probably already have or are planning a folder or notebook for each class you teach, a notebook that includes the class syllabus, individual lesson plans, and class assignments. This notebook will provide the foundation for the next time you teach the class, so the more complete it is, the easier your life will be in the future. The notebook reminds you exactly how you carried out the course. In our approach, we put all this material into a binder and ratchet up a notch or two the information we include. We include space for a running commentary that describes how things worked out in practice. If a planned fifteen-minute exercise ends up taking twenty-five minutes in practice, a note saying as much serves as a reminder to change the schedule next time around. If students dislike a particular text, but nonetheless find it useful, noting the content of the resistance and what students liked about the reading will help guide future students through the same assignment. If a colleague suggests a reading that would be perfect for a class, we make a note of the citation in the class's binder. Months after you've actually completed the class, you may have a realization of how you want to do things differently next time. Writing this up in the library will jog your memory at a later date.

The course-specific portion of the library helps you avoid having to start from scratch every time you teach a particular subject matter. At the same time, the library allows you to adjust a class over time without overhauling a class entirely. Because you're keeping track of what works and what doesn't as the class takes place, the library means you don't have to rely on faulty memory when you change out a reading or try a new lab assignment.

To repeat, the first part of the library entails a compilation of all those teaching tips. The second part of the archive entails a series of notebooks, folders, binders, or electronic files in which you group together information pertaining to particular classes. As time goes by, you'll turn to the library to solve problems that arise in your teaching or to refresh a class that feels a bit stale. You might encounter a student for whom your usual skills just aren't doing the trick. The teaching library will give you new ideas to communicate the lesson. Overall, these personal archives serve to organize your learning about teaching, reduce the expansive material on teaching to topics most relevant to you, and provide you with an accessible, tailor-made guide for your future work.

TO DO LIST

1. Remember, be fair, firm, and professional with your students.
2. Build a network of supporters who can give you the help you need.
3. Find out your school's requirements for earning tenure.
4. Find an extracurricular activity in which you're interested.
5. Explore continuing education possibilities.
6. Build a teaching library.

Conclusion

The Continuing Journey

A brief introductory text may not turn you into the consummate professional, but we hope you have been able to use advice throughout the book to grow as a teacher. Even at the same school, in the same department, no two instructors are the same, nor do they have the same needs. Our objective has been to offer a variety of ideas from which you can begin to develop your own formula for greatness. Where do you go once you have the basics covered?

Once you've identified a teaching style that works best for you, start exploring the extensive writing on the topic. Create a teaching support group that supports you in your quest. Teachers are passionate about educational philosophies and teaching techniques. Library and bookstore shelves reflect this passion. There are more than enough resources out there to keep you updated on teaching methods and trends in your subject area. As time goes by, don't be afraid to try new techniques and redefine your teaching style. Instead of settling into a comfort zone, we challenge you to keep pushing the envelope.

Writing on exceptional college teachers, Ken Bain says that "teaching is one of those human endeavors that seldom benefits from its past" (2004, 3). Although pedagogical trends and academic priorities shift over time, good teachers always find a way to connect to their students. As Bain suggests, we can never learn enough from others' experiences. Surround yourself with a community of teachers who care. Remember to include teachers from across the generational spectrum. Reach out to teachers whose background differs from your own in ethnicity, gender, or social class. Consider how their different perspectives can enrich your work with students.

You'll soon find that what really makes lifelong teaching possible is lifelong learning and lifelong sharing. Bon voyage!

References

Bain, Ken. 2004. *What the Best College Teachers Do*. Cambridge: Harvard University Press.

Bayard, Robert T. and Jean Bayard. 1986. *How to Deal with Your Acting Up Teenager: Practical Help for Desperate Parents*. New York: M. Evans and Company, Inc.

Ingersoll, Richard. 2001. *Teacher Turnover, Teacher Shortages, and the Organizations of Schools*. Seattle: Center for the Study of Teaching and Policy, University of Washington.

Rotenberg, Robert. 2007. *The Art and Craft of College Teaching: A Guide for New Professors and Graduate Students*. Walnut Creek, CA: Left Coast Press.

About the Authors

Eric J. Johnson is an assistant professor of bilingual education in the College of Education at Washington State University, Tri-Cities. He received his doctoral degree (2008) and master's degree (2005) in sociocultural anthropology from Arizona State University. He completed a master's degree in education (2000) at Northern Arizona University, with a specialization in secondary instruction and curriculum. After graduating from Western Washington University in 1997 with a B.A. and his Washington State K–12 Teaching Certificate, Dr. Johnson moved to Arizona where he worked as an educator at the high school, middle school, and elementary levels. He has taught Spanish, ESL, social studies, math, science, and language arts. At the post-secondary level, he has taught courses in Spanish, anthropology, and bilingual education. Currently, he works with pre-service and in-service teachers who are working toward a teaching endorsement in English as a second language and bilingual education. His research interests include immigrant education programs and language policy and planning.

Nora Haenn is associate professor of anthropology and international studies at North Carolina State University. She received both her doctoral degree (1998) and master's degree (1994) from Indiana University. Her undergraduate degree in philosophy (1989) is from Fordham University, a private school where class size topped out at thirty students and lecture and seminar courses were the norm. In her teaching career, Haenn has taught at regional and large state universities both on-line and in face-to-face settings, in class sizes ranging from three to eighty students. After a challenging start in college teaching, she decided to write the book she wished she'd read at the beginning of the journey.